DAVID BECKHAM *In Their Own Words*

Jo Stevenson

Becks
"Talking"

OMNIBUS PRESS

BECKS *Talking*

Cover & Book designed by Fresh Lemon.
Picture research by Sarah Bacon.

ISBN: 1.84449.167.6
Order No: OP49973

Exclusive Distributors:
Music Sales Limited,
8/9 Frith Street, London W1D 3JB, UK.

Music Sales Corporation,
257 Park Avenue South, New York, NY 10010, USA.

Macmillan Distribution Services,
53 Park West Drive, Derrimut, Vic 3030, Australia.

To the Music Trade only:
Music Sales Limited,
8/9 Frith Street, London W1D 3JB, UK.

Printed by: Caligraving Limited, Thetford, Norfolk.

A catalogue record for this book is available from the British Library.

Visit Omnibus Press on the web at www.omnibuspress.com

CONTENTS

My grateful thanks and appreciation goes to the following
publications/TV companies for providing source material:
*BBC, Big!, Daily Express, Daily Mail, Daily Star, Daily Telegraph,
Entertainment Weekly, Esquire, Evening Standard (London), GMTV, Hello!,
ITN, News Of The World, Q, Sky One, Sky Sports, Sunday Mirror,
Sunday Sport, The Sun, Time Out, Just Seventeen, Live And Kicking Magazine,
Marie Claire, Metro, Ms. London, Now, OK! Sunday Express,
Sunday Telegraph, The Guardian, The Independent, The Mirror,
The Observer, The Tatler, Vogue.*

Particular thanks to *Heat, The Michael Parkinson Show,
There's Only One David Beckham* and the inimitable Chris Charlesworth.

I must also express all due appreciation to the following websites:
BBC News, BBC Sport, virgin.net, soccernet.com, sportinglife.com,
and *Virtual Manchester*

All thanks to those whose views are included in this book, and of course,
a special big thank you to David Beckham himself.

ACKNOWLEDGEMENTS

If you were to take a hundred people at random throughout and the world and ask them to name a soccer player, 99 of them would respond instantly with the same reply – David Beckham.

David's achievements as a footballer are immense. Six English league titles, two FA Cups and a Champions League winner's medal are an apt reward for the player who can bend it like no-one else. He has captained the England team from the front for the last three seasons; images of his last-gasp equaliser against Greece and the penalty that sank Argentina at the 2002 World Cup finals have become some of the most memorable in English football history.

Introduction

All this would have made a racy enough story in its own right, but *Becks "Talking"* is much more than a footballer's tale. No other player has married a member of the world's biggest pop phenomenon of the Nineties or used his athleticism and good looks to become the leading male style icon on the planet. No-one else has shed the lager-'n'-lad lifestyle of most footballers for one that has raised questions of fashion, sexuality and the role of the modern male. Movie titles bear his name, in the last decade he has been immortalised in celluloid, wax and even oils more than any man alive.

Becks "Talking" rides the whole, amazing rollercoaster. In David's own words and those of family, friends and commentators, this is the story of how the lad from Leytonstone became the most famous man in the world.

Foot In The Door

DAVID ON SCHOOLDAYS, APPRENTICESHIPS AND JOINING UNITED...

"My mum and dad are the reason I'm the person I am today. They got me here. Yes, I worked hard, but they're the reason."

"When I was a kid, I lived for the game. The football was the first thing I got out when I got up and the last thing I put away before I went to bed. I just couldn't get enough... it didn't matter to me whether it was Wembley Stadium or a piece of parkland near our home in Chingford."

"As a kid, I used to run around my local park pretending I was Manchester United skipper, Bryan Robson, scoring goals. He was my idol."

"I would play football on my own for hours – or else with my dad... all my dad and I talk about is football!"

"When I was young, my dad always used to encourage my football. That's something I'll try and do with my own son, should he wish it."

"Even as a boy, I always tried to strike the ball properly. I have seen videos of me when I was six or seven doing just that."

“When I was young, I used to whack the free kicks. They'd go over the keepers' heads because they were so little.”

“I've always had willpower. And I've always said that when my mates were down the road, standing on the corner drinking cider, I was at home watching *Match Of The Day*.”

“Nothing ever distracted me from my football.”

“Running has always been part of me. I was 1,500 metres Champion at school for four years on the trot, and I used to do cross-country competitions which I loved. In fact, I used to get more nervous doing those runs than I ever do playing in front of 50,000 people.”

“If you stuck a girl or a ball in front of David he'd pick up the ball.”
JOHN BULLOCK, DAVID'S SPORTS TEACHER

“I think it's important to remove the idea that football is an exclusively male domain. When I was at school, some of the girls were as good as the boys. Getting girls involved might help to remove some of the macho nonsense that mars the game.”

“Loads of kids want to become professional footballers and you just can't blame them. (You're) in the fantastic position of being able to say 'My job is my hobby'”

FOOT IN THE DOOR

❝I don't know what I would have done if I didn't have football. I always enjoyed drawing, so maybe I'd something in art. But football was always number one.❞

❝I dreamt a lot about football and a lot of those dreams came true for me.❞

❝My mum and dad gave me all the advice I needed. But in the end, they left the big decision up to me – whether it was to (apprentice) with Manchester United, or to stay in London and play for Tottenham or Arsenal. They never said 'We support Manchester United, so you're going up there'. I think that was important, because if you're pushed into something, you go the other way.❞

❝Signing that piece of paper was just brilliant.❞
DAVID RECALLS THE MOMENT HE SIGNED AS A TRAINEE FOR MANCHESTER UNITED

❝Sir Bobby Charlton said I was the best eleven year old he'd seen in the six years of running his school.❞

❝David Beckham was unusual. He was desperate to be a footballer. His mind was made up when he was nine or ten. Many kids think that it's beyond them. But you can't succeed without practising at any sport.❞ **SIR BOBBY CHARLTON**

❝My belief is practice makes perfect. If I didn't practice, I suppose I wouldn't be able to put the ball on a sixpence as often as I do. When you don't get it right, you just have to practice some more...❞

"From day one, his talent had to be seen to be believed."

MANCHESTER UNITED YOUTH COACH, ERIC HARRISON

"I know when the ball was going in. I was always able to hit them like that, even as a kid. But I used to practice them back then too. That's why they come off." DAVID ON THE ART OF FREE KICKS

"When I came up to Manchester I stayed in the halls of residence and played football every single day for two weeks. It was my idea of heaven."

"I watched David Beckham develop at Manchester United, and none of the senior players had any doubt about how big he would be. Now his reputation precedes him."

FORMER MANCHESTER UNITED CAPTAIN BRYAN ROBSON

"We used to bring David to our games in London. He was our mascot at West Ham when he was only twelve."

MANCHESTER UNITED MANAGER ALEX FERGUSON

"I couldn't get enough of United as a kid, I knew it was the club for me."

"The opportunities are even better now than when I was a kid. But if you don't enjoy your football you can have the best facilities in the world and it doesn't count for anything."

"I never refuse to sign an autograph, because I know how I felt as a kid when I was turned down."

"My ambition is to stay at Manchester United, become captain and be the best player in the world..."

FOOT IN THE DOOR

Red Devil, White & Blue

DAVID BECKHAM'S THOUGHTS ON PLAYING FOR MANCHESTER UNITED AND ENGLAND, HIS TEAM MATES, FOOTBALLING TACTICS AND THE WILL TO WIN...

"The current Manchester United side has grown up together as friends. We trust each other and that comes out on and off the field. All the players who have joined the side over the years have slotted into that unit and created a togetherness."

"Gary Neville's my best friend. Out of all the Manchester United players, I get on best with him. We socialise a lot. To be honest, I think he's one of England's, no... Europe's, no... the *world*'s best right backs. I'm not just saying that because he's my mate, but because I personally think he's a great player."

"When David wants you to kick the ball he yells "It it', which sounds really funny. Then when you get into the back of his car, he says 'Don't scuff me levver'. We're always imitating him, but he doesn't mind. He just laughs." MANCHESTER UNITED TEAM MATE RYAN GIGGS

"I only have to open my mouth and I get slaughtered!"
DAVID DESCRIBES THE DIFFICULTY OF HAVING A COCKNEY ACCENT IN MANCHESTER

RED DEVIL, WHITE & BLUE

 **BECKS** *Talking*

"Ryan's a very easy going bloke. And what a great player!"

"Our captain, Roy Keane, is quite mischievous. He can play a few jokes on you. He's a very funny bloke with a dry sense of humour. He can say things and you just crease up. Great bloke."

"Andy Cole's an excellent finisher and an asset to Manchester United. Off the pitch, he's a friendly fella too, with a nice Cockney sense of humour."

"It's like Christmas coming every Saturday."
MANCHESTER UNITED STRIKER ANDY COLE ON DAVID'S PASSING ABILITY

"If we work hard, then the manager can't ask for much more. When every player on the pitch works hard, you are going to get a break in the end."

"I think I can do as much with my career with Manchester United as would be possible with any foreign club. With the trophies you get here, it's enough for any player to ask for. I think I can get all the satisfaction from (Manchester United) that I need... I don't need to look elsewhere."

"Every new season is big for me. I go into each one wanting to win everything."

"It's always important for us to get our first game out of the way with a win."

"Shopping!" **DAVID RESPONDS TO A QUESTION ABOUT HIS STRENGTHS**

"A win is a win. The win is all important."

"I wish I had scored that goal or one like it. It was one of those goals every player would like to score and David took it very well." ERIC CANTONA ON THE GOAL THAT ANNOUNCED BECKHAM TO A WIDER AUDIENCE, A 50-YARDER AGAINST WIMBLEDON IN 1996

❝I dream a lot about football and a lot of them have come true for me.**❞**

❝I love scoring goals, especially important ones. A lot of the time they go to other players, so it's nice to score goals... and get an ovation.❞

❝I look after myself. I eat well, I sleep well. It's important to look after your body – if you take care of yourself off the pitch it sees you all right on the pitch.**❞**

❝If we keep going, we'll get our just desserts.❞
DAVID ON MANCHESTER UNITED'S WINNING STRATEGY

❝I won the Double at 21 years old and that's unbelievable. But it didn't just doesn't end there.**❞**

❝Manchester United... The Heroes Who United A Nation.❞
THE DAILY MAIL

❝Records are made to be broken.**❞**
DAVID'S COMMENT AFTER MANCHESTER UNITED WON A UNIQUE TREBLE IN MAY 1999

❝Tackling is my weakest point. I've never been good at it. I'm always late or I mistime it.❞

❝I'm quite a confident person, but I do get nervous. Then... I relax.**❞**

RED DEVIL, WHITE & BLUE

"I get a bit annoyed when it's said I can't use my left foot. Most players can only stand on theirs. Mine's a bit better than that."

"My nan loves to watch me on TV, but is always saying how often I seem to argue with referees. Worse than that is the fact that my nan is an excellent lip-reader. She knows *exactly* what I'm saying."

"It's nice to see boys and girls walking down the street with 'Beckham' shirts and the number seven on their back. It makes me smile when I see that."

"If I do get into scrapes sometimes, I put that down to a certain side of my game but it's not one I want to lose, as it's a part of me."

"I just want to win everything all of the time. That's why some of these things happen. I don't do it maliciously, it's just my will to win."

"The opportunities are even better now than when I was a kid, but if you don't enjoy your football you can have the best facilities in the world and it doesn't count for anything."

"Loads of kids want to become professional footballers and you can't blame them. I'm in the fantastic position of being able to say my job is my hobby."

"He's one of the lads. Kevin Keegan. You know where you stand with him. Instead of sitting at the front of the coach, he'll sit with the lads.**"**

"David is the best crosser of a ball in Europe. The best striker of a dead ball I have *ever* come across. He's totally outstanding."

MANCHESTER UNITED MANAGER SIR ALEX FERGUSON

David on his relationship with Sir Alex...

"I would like to stay in the game when I eventually finish playing, but I don't think I'd fancy management. There's just too much hassle...**"**

"From the first day I came to the club Sir Alex has been like a father figure to me. He's been exactly what any player would need. Someone to look up to. He's also told me when I've done things right, and when I've done things wrong. Most importantly, he has given me the confidence to become the player I am. Obviously, everyone can have an occasional disagreement with his boss, and I've had one or two since I've been at the club."

"The fact is when I've had the odd disagreement with Sir Alex, it's been made into a crisis by the papers because it's *me*. But we've always got on and there's never been any real problem.**"**

SIR ALEX FERGUSON

RED DEVIL, WHITE *&* **BLUE**

❝It doesn't matter how high a player's profile is. If he is in the wrong, he is in the wrong, and David was definitely in the wrong. Nicky Butt, Phil Neville and Ole Gunnar Solskaer cannot count on being regulars in the first team, but they are model players who never miss training. (It was not) a satisfactory reason for being absent.❞ SIR ALEX ON TEMPORARILY DROPPING DAVID FROM THE MANCHESTER UNITED TEAM WHEN HE MISSED TRAINING. ACCORDING TO BECKHAM, HIS SON, BROOKLYN, WAS ILL AND NEEDED HIS FATHER

❝The papers are a danger for David. I try to protect him... make him stay down to earth. Or else.❞ **SIR ALEX FERGUSON**

❝All my impressions of Sir Alex Ferguson are that he's a nice man and he's really good at his job. But I don't think he realises that when he says (he has) problems with David, it's me who has to put up with the negativity.❞ VICTORIA ON SIR ALEX

❝The players know I don't hold any grudges. I haven't got time to hold any grudges.❞

❝What do I call him? Sir...❞ DAVID BECKHAM ON HIS MANAGER

❝The bottom line is that, for all the ups and downs, you know that he is making his football decisions for the right reasons❞
DAVID'S ASSESSMENT OF SIR ALEX IN HIS AUTOBIOGRAPHY, MY WORLD

"Nobody should underestimate David Beckham. I do like to have players as they grow up but it is impossible not to admire his resolve. It has served me well on many occasions. When the chips are down on the football field, you can bet your life that David Beckham won't be found wanting."

SIR ALEX PLACES HIS HIGH OPINION OF DAVID ON THE RECORD IN HIS AUTOBIOGRAPHY

David on his England captaincy and World Cup 2002...

"What has playing for Manchester United got to do with playing for your country?"

"I dream of playing in the centre for England. That's where I think I can give my best. I'm dream of playing in Paul Gascoigne's spot and to see my soccer have as much effect on the national team as Paul's did."

DAVID TRAINING WITH THE ENGLAND SQUAD   **RED DEVIL, WHITE & BLUE**

"Achieving what I have at Manchester United has been amazing, but winning something with England can only add to it. But I've still got a lot to learn at international level as well as at club level."

"Obviously I'd like to score more goals for England. Who wouldn't?"

"Inevitably, there are confrontations that take place from week to week with club sides, but you can't afford to hang on to them when you arrive in the national team."

"The goal has been a long time coming and I hope I don't have to wait three years for the next one. I didn't know what to do when I scored so I just ran over and jumped on Teddy Sheringham's back as he was warming up on the touch-line. It might have taken a bit of a deflection but they all count." DAVID DESCRIBES HIS MATCH-WINNING STRIKE IN A VITAL WORLD CUP QUALIFIER V FINLAND, MARCH 2001

"I looked for the best player in the squad to captain the England team, and there was only one choice: David Beckham. The way he handled himself, especially after the Argentina game was superb. He demonstrated how strong a character he was. I said to him: 'I'm making you skipper', and I don't think I gave him the option of turning it down." **FORMER ENGLAND COACH, PETER TAYLOR**

"I got the phone call one morning from Peter Taylor to tell me I was captain of the full squad. It took a minute or so or it to sink in. Everyone knows what happened three years ago, so to come through it like that was great."

RED DEVIL, WHITE & BLUE

❝I was so proud of David. It was amazing when we found out he was going to be England captain. I'll always support him in everything he does.**❞** VICTORIA

❝I was very nervous the first time I was made England captain. Everyone said I wasn't up to the job. Obviously, I had a lot to prove. But whatever people throw at me, I'll keep trying to make them think again. Now, I want to stay England captain for the rest of my career. I don't want to play for my country again and not wear that armband - I love the responsibility. Being England skipper is an unbelievable feeling, the best I've ever had in football. When you've done the job once, you never want to let it go...❞

❝David Beckham is respected by the coaches, the manager and his team-mates. I would be surprised if the job of England captain went to anyone else in the next few years.**❞**

FORMER ENGLAND COACH, PETER TAYLOR

❝I'd never ever been a senior captain before – apart from one game at Manchester united when no-one wanted to do it.❞

❝David Beckham can make a good England captain. More than anything else, you need the respect of your fellow team-mates, and he certainly has that. Some lead by grabbing people by the scruff of the neck, and giving them a good kick up the backside. Others can be just as good with a well-chosen word here and there.

WITH SVEN GORAN ERIKSSON

Perhaps (David) will lead by example, scoring a good goal, making a crucial tackle, passing a great ball. You influence people by what you do on the pitch. **" FORMER ENGLAND CAPTAIN TERRY BUTCHER**

"To be made captain of the England team when we're doing so well is one of the greatest honours I could have been given in football. "

"David doesn't waste energy. You don't see him ducking or diving or throwing tantrums like some wingers. He whips the ball in first time. That means he doesn't waste energy going past his man.**" FORMER ENGLAND MANAGER, KEVIN KEEGAN**

"It's a challenge to play football against the best players in the world. And it's also a chance to stake a claim for myself. "

"Everyone knows how well England are doing. Manchester United must do the same**"**

"I think he was a very good choice for England captain. I also think maybe he's the most famous footballer in England... perhaps even the world. Every football fan knows who David Beckham is. He sets a very good example, and so far, has done very, very well. I hope it's going to be for a long time. "
CURRENT ENGLAND COACH, SVEN GORAN ERIKSSON

"Sven Goran Eriksson is such a calm man, such a calming influence. The players are so relaxed around him.**"**

RED DEVIL, WHITE & BLUE

"We've reached a stage where we're in with a real chance of going to the World Cup and not being scared of anyone – not even the French. After beating Germany 5-1, we don't have to worry about any other country. Believe me, there's a lot more to come from this team."

"I'll be a failure if I don't lift a trophy as England captain. Success with the national team is an absolute must."

"People have said 2002 is too early for the England team to go to the World Cup and do really well. I don't agree. I've had success all the way with Manchester United and that feeling is immense. Now I *have* to bring that to this England team."

"When you follow David's career in the papers, you read a lot about his wife and so on, but you don't really get to know him as a person. And I must say David is a big, big professional, a big, big captain. He's shown that by his performances."

SVEN GORAN ERIKSSON

"I want youngsters to look up to me and copy the things I do on the pitch for England and United. The most important I learned in the early days was to enjoy my football, and that's what I'm trying to pass on to kids today."

"We've all dreamed of winning the World Cup, and I'm no different to anyone else..."

Footballers old and new offer their opinion on David's gift...

66 David Beckham works harder than any footballer I've ever seen on a pitch. He never gives up. 99 **GEORGE BEST**

66 **There's so much more to David Beckham than we've seen so far.** 99

KEVIN KEEGAN

66 David must take it as a compliment that other teams close him down so much. They do it because they fear him. 99 **BRYAN ROBSON**

66 **He can put a ball on someone's head from fifty yards.** 99

PAUL MERSON

WITH MICHAEL OWEN

66 There's not many people who work as hard as David Beckham. 99 **MICHAEL OWEN**

66 **David Beckham has won the respect and admiration of everyone because of the way he has conducted himself on and off the pitch. Everybody loves him and so they should. But the transformation (since World Cup '98) is in the way the country thinks about him is solely down to him. David Beckham really is 'King Becks'.** 99

ENGLAND/LEEDS GOALKEEPER NIGEL MARTYN

66 I don't think you realise quite how good he is until you play alongside him. He can do so many things with a football. He's got the world at his feet. 99 **ALAN SHEARER**

RED DEVIL, WHITE & BLUE 99

❝I'm always being compared with Ryan Giggs but I can't see it myself. I was more David Beckham. Giggs' ratio of goals to games isn't good enough or his final ball. He's a terrific player but that Beckham, every so often he changes the game. Turns it on its head. Great player that.❞ GEORGE BEST

❝Beckham thrills me. He is one of the elite players in Europe. He is truly gifted. When my son Jordi joined Manchester United a couple of years ago, he told me of Beckham's great abilities and I took notice... Beckham would have fitted into any team of mine, either in Spain or at Ajax in Holland. He is a fabulous crosser of the ball and possesses terrific skills.❞ **DUTCH LEGEND JOHAN CRUYFF**

❝It seems to me that he has learned a lesson that it also took me a while to fathom. The greatest hurt of all a player can inflict on a football field is through his ability. Beckham possesses the rare capability of not only being able to see the required pass but being able to deliver it.❞ EX-ENGLAND VETERAN TOM FINNEY

❝Beckham is brilliant. He is very good technically. He has great awareness, a great shot and of course he provides those fantastic crosses. I think the incident of temperament in the World Cup was a one-off.❞ **TOP ITALIAN COACH MARCELLO LIPPI**

❝He causes you problems because there is only one David Beckham but you need two in your team, A manager needs one David Beckham to play right wing, where he is better than anyone else, and one to play inside. If they ever start cloning footballers, he would be the first you sent to the laboratory.❞
KEVIN KEEGAN

❝David Beckham has been a brilliant role model for me. He has grown in stature since becoming captain and made life easier for all the young players in the England squad.❞
ENGLAND FULL-BACK ASHLEY COLE

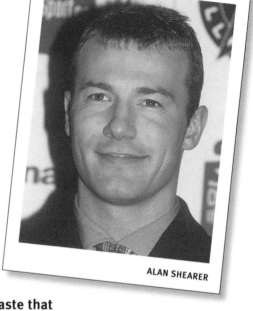

ALAN SHEARER

❝David Beckham is a suitable role model for every starry-eyed kid in the land.❞ THE SUN

❝A really fine player in every respect and he has two feet which a lot of people say players don't have these days.❞

JIMMY HILL

❝David Beckham is the best crosser of the ball I have ever seen and, in my opinion, you don't waste that sort of ability...David is the perfect outlet for any team because his positional sense is so good.❞ ALAN SHEARER

❝I think so highly of Beckham. He could be the Cantona of United and reach similar heights with England.❞ GEORGE BEST

❝Obviously, it's nice for people to talk like that, but if I listen too much, I start worrying. I just have to switch off from all the fame and acclaim... I have to focus on not getting big headed about it. Obviously, there is praise and adulation, but it's all about keeping my feet on the ground and having good people around me.❞

And finally, Victoria's views on a national obsession...

❝You might not like the team David plays for, but you can't dispute the fact he's a fantastic footballer.❞

"There aren't any other footballers I particularly fancy. I've got the best one, haven't I?"

"I call what David does football competitions. I can never remember what they're supposed to be called. Football games? Football matches! Oh well, it's all a performance, innit?"

"I don't think Victoria knows about the off-side rule..." DAVID

"I know what a goal is, which is surely the most important thing in football, but I don't know about the offside rule, or stuff like that."

"I'm not the football wife type. I don't even know the rules of football."

"Actually, some footballer's wives are really intelligent. A lot of them have degrees. I suppose you might get one or two who might be a bit divvy, but it's the same in every walk of life."

"I'm not a football fan, but I like to watch David. But I'd be bored to death if I had to watch a game and he wasn't playing in it."

"I like David for him, and I don't care what he does as long as it makes him happy."

RED DEVIL, WHITE & BLUE

Spice Up Your Life

DAVID AND VICTORIA RECOUNT THEIR FIRST MEETING, SUBSEQUENT ENGAGEMENT AND WEDDING IN JULY 1999...

"I first saw Victoria on the telly and I wanted to meet her. I knew I fancied her. So then it was just a case of getting together."

"I always used to go for blondes and quiet girls but Victoria is the total opposite – dark and loud."

"He pointed at the TV and said 'That's the girl for me, and I'm going to get her.'" DAVID'S BEST FRIEND, MANCHESTER UNITED'S GARY NEVILLE

"Actually, I fancied David long before I met him. I remember doing an interview with a magazine and they showed me photographs of loads of different footballers. I remember seeing David and thinking one word: 'Gorgeous'. I decided to stalk him."

"When we did first meet, I wanted to sound like I knew something about football. So I said something like, 'Good game then?' He just laughed, and that was it. I just knew."

"As soon as I met Victoria, I knew I was going to marry her. I had a sneaky feeling she might come to another game. I just couldn't stop thinking about her." DAVID

SPICE UP YOUR LIFE

❝I wasn't attracted by David's fame, but as we got to know each other, we realised it was a great bonus. We were equally famous.❞

❝I liked Victoria for herself. I'd have liked her if she worked in Tesco.❞

❝On our first date, we were thrown out of a Chinese restaurant in Chingford because neither of us wanted to eat. We'd gone there to find somewhere where we could have a quiet drink without being noticed. We actually ended in Mel C's flat.❞ VICTORIA

❝David was quite the groupie. After taking me out, he bought a Spice Girls CD to do some research.❞

❝At first, David made no attempt to kiss me. But afterwards, he showered me with roses and a black Prada handbag. And I like a man who opens doors, takes me out to dinner and buys me flowers.❞

❝I starting thinking about proposing marriage a week after I met her.❞

❝I knew David liked me, but after three dates he still hadn't kissed me. He finally got round to it when we were at my parents' house. It was worth the wait.❞

❝If you're a bloke, you go out and mess about with girls. It's (seen) as quite a cool thing to do. David has made it cool to be the opposite, really. You forever read about celebrities having affairs, but we're *not* like that.❞

❝Since I've got to know her I love her more and more.❞

❝Before David Beckham, you thought of footballers as getting drunk, drinking beer... going out on the town. Not now.❞

LADY VICTORIA HERVEY

66David can't understand why the papers are so fascinated by his private life. My reply to that is 'Well don't go out with a Spice Girl!'99

TEAM-MATE BRIAN MCCLAIR

66At the start of our relationship, we were flying all over the place just to be with each other for an hour.99 DAVID

66David is an animal in bed.99 **VICTORIA**

66I doubt when David wakes up next to me... he thinks he is lying next to one of the sexiest women in the world, because when I wake up I look shocking!99

66I couldn't be happier. I've now got my dream woman.99

66I call what he does football competitions. I can never remember what they're supposed to be.99

VICTORIA ADMITS TO A SLENDER GRASP OF FOOTBALL

66I like him for him and I don't care what he does as long as it makes him happy.99

66We've been asked to do *Playboy* together, me and Victoria, as a pair. I don't think I'll ever go naked but I'll never say never.99

66While I was in America, we decided we'd get engaged. I'd already told him what my dream ring would be, and he'd remembered and had it specially designed for me. So, we were sitting there in our pyjamas when David pulled out the ring, got down on one knee

SPICE UP YOUR LIFE

and said: 'Will you marry me, Victoria?' I said: 'Yes', then produced my own ring and said: 'Don't forget Girl Power... will you marry me?'

David was everything I ever wanted in a person. We genuinely love each other. We're very good friends and very honest. I've found the man I going to get old and wrinkly with. Well, looks aren't going to last forever, are they?

David's very honest with me and sometimes the truth hurts. But I like that - I don't want to be surrounded by 'Yes' people.

It's been a great year. I'm getting married and my football club won The Treble.

I can honestly say I don't fancy anyone but David. Honestly.

I'm with someone I love and want to spend the rest of my life with. BECKS DECLARES HIS LOVE FOR VICTORIA

Neither of us are particularly religious. Perhaps we're more spiritual than religious.

If I'd had a more low key wedding, I would have been called a tight cow. As it is, people say we're flash and over the top. Well, that's fine. But I know we had the most amazing day.

When we got to the actual wedding venue, we helped Victoria in with her big dress and David was actually in tears. It was all very moving. **VICTORIA'S STYLIST, KENNY HO**

My best man, Gary Neville, was nervous... worrying about the speech, the ring, everything.

I remember the thrones. That was... different.

ALAN HANSEN

"Sitting on a throne. What's that all about?" ULRIKA JOHNSON

"I think there was an element of irony to David and Victoria's wedding that went over some people's heads...**"** ANGUS DEAYTON

"Our earnings are often exaggerated. When you read in a newspaper: 'Exclusive interview!' they think we've been paid a lorry load of cash. But we really get nothing. Only once, when we sold the rights to our wedding pictures for £1.2 million to *OK!* magazine. We did that to get rid of the paparazzi, and also to have nice wedding pictures. The money was spent on wedding preparations and security. Everything left over, we gave to charity, but I still get flak about how much we earned." VICTORIA

"On a regular month, *OK!* would sell between 500,000 and 600,000 copies. Just the first issue covering David and Victoria's wedding sold nearly 2 *million* copies. In fact, we nearly sold 5 million copies in a month.**"** MARTIN TOWNSEND, FORMER EDITOR, *OK!*

"It was such a fabulous day." DAVID

"The fact is, we wouldn't have done the wedding any differently. Everything went to plan. We could have had lots of celebrities wandering around who didn't really know us, but we did it our way and we don't regret a thing. Our wedding was a fairytale... a dream come true.**"** **VICTORIA**

"I wasn't actually invited to the wedding. I'm still fairly disappointed about that..." GARY LINEKER

"I kept hearing Victoria saying 'This is my husband'.**"** **DAVID**

"I just wanted to say 'I have you. I'm now Victoria Beckham. I'm quite old-fashioned like that." VICTORIA

SPICE UP YOUR LIFE

"I just love the fact I have the same surname as David. I feel much more... famous now. Everyone knows the name Beckham, so it's a wonderful feeling. But I haven't had time to practice my signature yet.**"**

"The honeymoon was so romantic. I felt so relaxed. In the end, we only had four days. But it was lovely because it was just the three of us. Brooklyn came too. We just couldn't bear to be parted from him."

"I think David gets more respect (from people than me), because he's considered more talented.**"**

"David just gets so frustrated sometimes because people think because he doesn't say a lot, he's stupid. But he's actually really smart. Very... deep and spiritual." VICTORIA

"It does hit hard if you're being told every day you can't sing or you can't dance. And that's exactly what I was being told by the media on a daily basis. I'd had enough of it really. Then David began to build up my confidence.**"**

“David was the backbone behind my album. He gave me the confidence to do it. When people say 'Can she sing?' or 'Can she do this or that?' I'm not going to lie, that knocks your confidence. But it was David who built up my confidence and said 'Get in there and do it. You want to do it. You love doing it.'”

“She wasn't confident about doing a solo album and needed a little push. So I gave her a little push.” DAVID

“Prince Charles asked me if David and I had any plans to do a duet. I said 'No way!'” VICTORIA

“Half the time when I see David I look anything but posh.”
VICTORIA ON BEING UPSTAGED BY HER HUSBAND

“There are two big ballads that I wrote for David on the LP – 'Unconditional Love' and 'IOU'. 'Unconditional Love' is a ballad all about our relationship, and 'IOU' explains that I wouldn't be where I am today without him. Like the song says 'I owe him everything... I'd be nothing without him'. I have really opened my heart.”

“I play her album in my car.” DAVID

“David's like a big brother to us and we want to support him all the way” MEL C

SPICE UP YOUR LIFE

A Chip Off The Old Beck

DAVID AND VICTORIA ON PREGNANCY, PARENTHOOD AND THE BIRTH OF THEIR SON, BROOKLYN IN MARCH, 1999

"I couldn't believe it when she told me.**"**

DAVID ON DISCOVERING HE'S GOING TO BE A DAD

"He hasn't stopped talking about the baby since the day I told him." VICTORIA

"I've always loved kids and I don't mind getting involved on the mucky side of things**" DAVID PREPARES TO ROLL HIS SLEEVES UP**

"One of David's most attractive qualities is he shares the same family values as me."

"I am totally ready for fatherhood. The happiest moment of my life was when Victoria told me she was pregnant. In fact, I was so over the moon, I was lost for words. And though the pregnancy wasn't planned, there wasn't a second of doubt in my mind. We both understand what having children involves and we're both ready for the responsibility.**"**

"David came in for the first scan and just cried and cried when he saw our baby. Whenever we talk about it, he just smiles... he says: 'You look lovely. You're just keeping our baby warm.' He's so sweet about it."

BROOKLYN WITH GRANDMA
(SANDRA BECKHAM)

A CHIP OFF THE OLD BECK

"Towards the end of my pregnancy, I was so huge. I'd sit in a chair positioned in front of the fridge, totally starkers with my massive belly. David used to pull me up from the chair, open the fridge so I could grab some food, then ease me back into the chair. He'd say: 'You look lovely, you know...'"

"A couple of nights before Brooklyn was born, my dad took me to one side and said "You know, when the baby's born and you first set eyes on him, you'll understand how your mother and I feel about you.'" DAVID

"Victoria kept on going on about how hungry she was!"

"I cried when Brooklyn was born. I wanted to cut his umbilical cord, but the doctor did it so quickly, I didn't get a chance." DAVID

"David was with me in the hospital when I had Brooklyn, and I was completely oblivious to the fact there were thousands of people outside until I turned on the TV and there were *GMTV* broadcasting from Portland Hospital. That completely freaked me out. David was supposed to stay the night in the room next door, but I made him make up a camp bed in my room, so that if anyone tried to get to Brooklyn, they'd have to trample over David's head first!"

"His name is Brooklyn Joseph, and we are both overjoyed. The birth was natural, and there were no complications, nothing at all. Victoria is very well. She's sitting up drinking champagne and has already spoken to the other Spice Girls."
DAVID MEETS THE PRESS FOLLOWING THE BIRTH OF HIS SON

"The baby is lovely, sitting in his Mum's arms. I am very pleased."

"David and I found out I was pregnant while I was on tour in America. We were actually in Brooklyn, New York."
VICTORIA EXPLAINS HOW BROOKLYN BECKHAM GOT HIS NAME

"He has got Victoria's nose, but he's also got my legs, my feet and my toes... *exactly* the same toes as me."

"As soon as I saw Brooklyn... he became the only thing that really mattered. Him and David. It instantly put my life into perspective. I love him so much it hurts. David feels the same. He's an amazing father."

"Fatherhood is the best thing that's ever happened to me. It's something that can't be beaten."

"I'm quite happy to sit up all night just watching Brooklyn breathe." DAVID

"David's much better at changing nappies than me."

"I've always loved kids, so I don't mind getting involved in the mucky side of things." DAVID

"David's bought a little baby Manchester United football shirt which says 'Beckham' on the back. Ahhhh." VICTORIA

"We always wanted a boy..." DAVID

A CHIP OFF THE OLD BECK

"Brooklyn loves to watch David play, and I like to see Brooklyn enjoying himself."
VICTORIA

"**I'd like Brooklyn to play for Manchester United, of course.**" TED BECKHAM, DAVID'S FATHER

"Brooklyn's a really good footballer. He's better than I was at his age. Well, my mum says he is, anyway. Even when he's got a load of toys, he always goes for the football first... it'll be interesting to see how he turns out. I'd love him to go into football." **DAVID**

"**Brooklyn's a handsome little fellow – just like his dad.**"
SANDRA BECKHAM, DAVID'S MOTHER

"David's not the greatest dancer. He'll kill me for (saying) this, but he can stand at the bar and sway about, and that's about it. Brooklyn was in my tummy in the studio and on tour, so I know he's definitely got rhythm. Imagine him at the school disco – a great footballer with good rhythm – he's going to have great pulling power..."

"**If Brooklyn sees David on the telly, he shouts 'Daddy! Daddy!' It must be a little strange for him really...**" VICTORIA

"Brooklyn has made me look at life from a whole new perspective. Things that seemed important before just don't seem as important now." **DAVID**

"Brooklyn is the best thing that's ever happened to me. Being a dad is more important than football."

"It really hurts when the crowds sing 'Is that baby really yours, Beckham?'"

"The reason fans abuse me is because they are jealous of me."

"There's been a lot of stuff in the press about people wanting to kidnap Brooklyn and I did have threats. But the police were fantastic. Brooklyn has a bodyguard with him now."

In November 2002, a story broke in the News of the World of an alleged kidnap plot against Victoria and the family. Although it was exposed as a hoax months later, it naturally had a profound effect on David and Victoria:

"I'm in absolute and total shock. It's clear these people were serious and that, of course, has scared the life out of me." VICTORIA

A CHIP OFF THE OLD BECK

❝It really was horrendous. I was being driven around in bullet-proof cars, I wasn't allowed to go out of the house. We had police sitting outside the house.❞ VICTORIA

❝There have been many stories saying we're selling pictures of Brooklyn, and they're all untrue. I get really angry when I read that stuff because we've never even considered it. We don't want his picture splashed all over the papers. If he wants to do that stuff when he's older, that's his decision. But not now.❞ DAVID

❝People can say what they want about me. But David and Brooklyn, they're *mine*. They can't touch them.❞

❝I'm quite a relaxed bloke. I'll often let things go over my head rather than let them get to me. Sometimes, it's hard because the attention we get is 'full-on' every day. In fact, not a day goes by without something cropping up in the news about us. Yeah, it's hard, but it makes us a strong family – all three of us.❞

❝When Brooklyn grows up, we're both unfortunately aware he's never going to get any privacy in his life. It'll probably change from, 'What's happening with David and Victoria?' to 'What's Brooklyn doing?', 'Who's Brooklyn's first girlfriend?' or 'Brooklyn's first car'. But, as parents, we'll try and protect him as much as we can.❞ DAVID

❝My whole life took on a whole new meaning with the birth of our first son Brooklyn. It was a fantastic experience and taught me what real happiness is all about. I have much to be thankful for in my professional and private life. I am with the woman I love and we have a beautiful child. I play for the greatest football club in the world and have been blessed with the talent which enables me to play for my country.❞

Victoria and David's views on future additions to the Beckham household...

❝I think we'd like a couple more children, maybe. But I don't think I'd be able to fit any more names on the tongue of my boot! You see, I usually have the name 'Beckham' on the front of my boot, but now oit' 'Brooklyn' with 'Beckham' on the back. I think Adidas are quite pleased actually!❞

❝I can't put into words what I feel for Brooklyn. It's a bond between the three of us that started when he was growing in Victoria's womb. It's unbelievable. He's unbelievable. We're a family now.❞ DAVID

A CHIP OFF THE OLD BECK ❞❞

Argy Bargy
&Greece
Lightning

DAVID BECKHAM'S TWO MOST IMPORTANT GAMES: HIS SENDING OFF AGAINST ARGENTINA IN WORLD CUP '98, AND ENGLAND'S BATTLE WITH GREECE TO QUALIFY FOR WORLD CUP 2002...

Beckham's lowliest footballing moment surely came in World Cup '98. In a critical qualifying match against old adversaries, Argentina, he was sent off following a foul on Diego Simeone. Reduced to ten men, England subsequently lost the game, and exited the competition. What follows is a record of the incident and the effect it had on David's life...

❝I never looked forward to anything in my professional life as much as I did to World Cup '98. Like all football-mad kids, I grew up watching the greatest players on television battling it out for the biggest team prize in sport. What happened was... unfortunate.❞

❝It was like the Kennedy thing – 'Where were you the night the president was shot?' In Elizabethan times, Becks would have been sent to the Tower and had his feet chopped off!❞

RICHARD E. GRANT

ARGY BARGY & GREECE LIGHTNING

❝I was sitting on the England bench at the time. I saw David kick out at the Argentine and thought 'He's off'.**❞**

PAUL MERSON

❝I was shouting 'What are you doing? What are you doing?!'❞

SUPERMODEL JODIE KIDD

❝I couldn't believe the ref sent him off for such an innocent little kick.**❞**

GARY LINEKER

GARY LINEKAR

❝Let's just say the referee fell into a trap. It was a difficult decision to avoid because I went down well, and in moments like that, there's always tension. You could say my falling down transformed a yellow card into a red card. But in fact, the most appropriate punishment was a yellow card. Obviously, I was being clever. By letting myself fall, I got the referee to pull out a red card immediately. In reality, David's (kick) wasn't a violent blow. It was just a little kick with no force behind it... probably just instinctive. But the referee was right there and punished his intention to retaliate.❞

ARGENTINE INTERNATIONAL DIEGO SIMEONE, THE PLAYER DAVID 'KICKED'

❝The sending off was pretty straightforward. The rules are very clear about kicking or attempting to kick an opponent. In that type of situation, one person has to be punished. If I hadn't has sent him off, I would have been punished for not following the rules. But I was quite surprised by the reaction after the game...**❞**

REFEREE KIM MILTON NEILSON

"That ref nearly ruined David's life. I actually don't know how Beckham coped with it. When you read the papers in the next few days, he'd been getting bullets in the post. I think I'd have moved to Outer Mongolia." PAUL MERSON

"Ten heroic lions, one stupid boy." DAIRY MIRROR HEADLINE

"It's generally safer to have nothing to do with journalists. They put unnecessary pressure on players, managers – even referees – and I find it hard to understand how people who claim to love the game of football try so hard to damage it." DAVID

"There's no need to look for scapegoats. David didn't do it on purpose, it's a mistake he made, and he will learn from that mistake. He's very upset about the whole thing, (because) he's realised the gravity of what he's done. He's still a young lad, and of course, all this criticism... is something that is going to be very hard for him to deal with." FORMER ENGLAND MANAGER GLENN HODDLE

"Of course I re-lived that moment. Two days before the Argentina game I was a hero. Then the next day, they wanted me hung. People can be so fickle."

"We will see an even better David Beckham because of this." MANCHESTER UNITED/ENGLAND TEAM MATE PHIL NEVILLE

"Because I went straight to America after World Cup
'98, my family bore the brunt of what was coming to me.
That was a big thing for them, because they're not used to that
sort of stuff. For normal people, handling 20 or 30 journalists
outside your door is definitely not something you're used to, and
my mum, dad and the rest of my family did amazingly well."

"The abuse that boy got..." ACTOR JAMES 'COLD FEET' NESBITT

"I suppose booing was (the fans') way of getting back at me."

"Actually, I feel safest *on* the field. Even though I can hear what
people are saying or chanting, I can concentrate... enjoy the game.
I can keep them quiet by scoring a goal."

"David does take a severe amount of people slagging him off.
Do they do that to Ronaldo in Italy? I don't think so. They put him
up on a pedestal and said 'Good bloke. You're a talented player
who works hard'. Then if he
went to (another country),
it'd be 'Oh, why is he
going?' Well, why do you
think?" VICTORIA

"At one point, I couldn't
see any light at the end of
the tunnel. There was
nothing I could say or do
to make it stop..."

"Obviously, it's going to be difficult when people are using your head as a dartboard..." VICTORIA

"What David had to go through was nothing short of scandalous. I couldn't understand it. People can say what they want about you off the pitch, but he answered everybody's with his performances *on* the pitch."

GARY NEVILLE

DAVID WITH GARY NEVILLE

"The shouts certainly didn't affect his football, because he was fantastic every time he put on a shirt for Manchester united or England." MICHAEL OWEN

"I just sat it out. That's always been my mentality. I'd had previous knocks in my career and I just wanted the opportunity to show people I could do my best – both for my club and my country."

"The past year must have been so hard to take for David. It's been a joke, and a sick one at that, the way he's been jeered every tie he got the ball. Yet, he's handled it brilliantly and is playing better than ever. I'd like to think we've all helped him. There are no superstars in our dressing room, so we all give him plenty of stick. That's the way it works with us – you take the mickey out of each other. A good laugh not only eases the strain but brings you all closer together." MANCHESTER UNITED TEAM MATE RYAN GIGGS

"The Manchester United players and fans never doubted me, and that's the reason I'm still here and playing well."

ARGY BARGY & **GREECE LIGHTNING**

"If I do get into scrapes sometimes, I put it down to a certain side of my game. But it's not one I want to lose, because it's part of me. I just want to win everything all the time. That's why some of these things happen. I don't do it maliciously. It's just my will to win."

"David has a wonderful skill and a wonderful attitude to the game. He wants to be a great footballer. Unfortunately, he sometimes falls foul of officialdom...and that's what happened here. Sadly, the consequences were enormous."

FORMER ENGLAND MANAGER GLENN HODDLE

"(In the end), the sending off made grow up, realise a few things about myself..."

"There is no way I would have survived the World Cup incident without Victoria. She didn't say anything, just gave me this big cuddle. She was about a month pregnant – and no-one knew but us. In the end, I think she was as pleased to see me as I was her. Once I was with her, I *knew* I'd get through it."

"Let's not forget, he's a fantastic footballer... which is the be all and end all." ALAN SHEARER

"England had a mountain of courage and a molehill of luck in that game. Unfortunately, of course, certain things happened that... shouldn't have happened." **PRIME MINISTER TONY BLAIR**

"I have seen the game many times on video since, and I would not change any of my decisions." REFEREE KIM MILTON NIELSEN

"When I'm feeling down about myself, thinking 'Why do people think that about me?' or 'Why are they saying that?' what better person can I look to than my own husband to see how someone can turn everything around?" VICTORIA

" What happened against Argentina does not still haunt me. I think a lot of people would like to think it still does. But you move on from these things. You have to, otherwise they can affect you. I've moved on now and I'm a stronger person for it. "

" He came back from the World Cup finals after making a mistake which any of us could have committed and the whole country was ready to bury him, but he has battled back and shown his maturity. He has answered the taunts, not verbally, but in the best way possible with his skill as a great footballer. **"** ALAN SHEARER

" According to the Argentine players, Beckham's kick was the worst they had ever seen. According to the English players, it was nothing. There's war in the world... people dying everywhere. Yet, in England, the biggest problem is one player who made a small mistake in a football match. I think that's bad. "

KIM MILTON NIELSON

" There are more important things in life than football. " DAVID

The World Cup Qualifier

On October 8th, 2002, England played Greece at Old Trafford. If they won or drew the game, the team would automatically qualify for the World Cup finals in 2002. David Beckham's contribution to the match assured him a place in footballing history...

"This is the game, that if we win, means we're through to the World Cup. That means a massive amount to the players. We also know it means a lot to the entire nation. But we've not worked so hard in the last few months to lose this game. It's in our hands, so we can make it or break it." **DAVID**

"We didn't play that well, especially in the first half. Greece deserved 1-0 at half time." ENGLAND MANAGER SVEN GORAN ERIKSSON

"We couldn't get our tempo going. The crowd got upset. We got upset. It made us panicky. We just had to dig deep, and I think the captain showed us how. David ran his feet into the ground, gave a tremendous performance. He deserved everything."
ENGLAND GOAL-SCORER TEDDY SHERINGHAM

"Teddy's a nice bloke... and a great player. We're both cockneys so we understand each other!" DAVID

"David Beckham raised that England team by its' bootlaces in the last fifteen minutes..." *MATCH OF THE DAY*'S **MARK LAWRENCESON**

"Beckham lines up for the free kick. Is this one of those moments?" MARTIN TYLER

"Great players rise to great occasions..."
HENRY WINTER, THE DAILY TELEGRAPH

ARGY BARGY & **GREECE LIGHTNING**

❝As Becks put that ball down... I shouted to him, This is our last chance. He knew he had only 20 seconds to save us. He knew that if he didn't score, we were going through to the play-offs. But if anybody can cope with that kind of pressure, it's Becks.❞

ENGLAND DEFENDER GARY NEVILLE

❝I just couldn't bear the tension...❞ **JOANNE BECKHAM, DAVID'S SISTER**

JOANNE BECKHAM, DAVID'S SISTER

❝Luckily, we have the best player in the world at taking free kicks...❞

SVEN GORAN ERIKKSON

❝I knew this was my last throw of the dice...❞ **DAVID**

❝When he went up to take that free kick, I was willing him to score. I can't tell you how I felt when the ball went in. It was just fantastic... I was so proud of him.❞ VICTORIA

❝Yes, yes for England! David Beckham has done it!❞ **MARTIN TYLER**

❝To be honest, one *had* to go in. I'd had quite a few free kicks and was disappointed with most of them. But then, I got my chance. Teddy said to me 'I'll have it'. But I thought 'It's a bit too far out for him'. Somehow, I just fancied it... I had a good feeling.❞ DAVID

❝As soon as David scored, we knew we just had to wait it out for the final whistle...❞ **ENGLAND DEFENDER MARTIN KEOWN**

"When the game finally ended, every player on that pitch congratulated Beckham. A great goal. A tremendous player. An absolute hero."

FORMER ENGLAND STRIKER TREVOR BROOKING

"When you think about what he went through after being sent off against Argentina in World Cup '98, it was a phenomenal turnaround. As far as his England team-mates were concerned, he was certainly a king." ENGLAND GOALKEEPER, NIGEL MARTYN

"As a captain, David rose to the challenge. You could see the respect his team-mates have for him. He embodies everything good about English football." FOOTBALL ASSOCIATION CHIEF, ALAN CROZIER

"With David Beckham, everybody talks about the skill, but for me, it's the work. When England were struggling and needed a hero, he stood up and was counted. He is a role model on and off the field and a true captain." HENRY WINTER, THE DAILY TELEGRAPH

"In terms of drama, I have never witnessed anything like that match. We owe everything to David."

FORMER ENGLAND STRIKER, TREVOR FRANCIS

"David played one of the best games I have ever seen him play. He was a real captain for his country, and I'm so glad he scored that goal."

SVEN GORAN ERIKKSON

ARGY BARGY & **GREECE LIGHTNING**

"We didn't play the prettiest of games. They kept coming back and we just had to keep battling. But, as I've said before, the character of the players is unbelievable. For a young team to go 1-nil under, then equalise, go 2-1 down and then come back again...it just showed how much we wanted it." DAVID

"For England, it was a poor performance. But, in the way that great players do, David Beckham did everything. He worked harder than everyone... played better than everyone. At one point, he was taking on great clumps of Greek defenders on his own. It was quite extraordinary." PAUL HAYWARD, THE DAILY TELEGRAPH

"Greece made it a very difficult game for us. They're an extremely capable side. Yes, it was tough game, but we showed the necessary resolve to come through it."

ENGLAND DEFENDER RIO FERDINAND

"Now that the party's over, we have to be honest. It was a very poor England performance. Being fair to Greece, both of England's goals came from free kicks given for non-existent fouls. Cheating, basically. But that said, I still feel England has a very good chance of wining the next World Cup." PATRICK BARCLAY, THE SUNDAY TELEGRAPH

"The referee gave a festival of free kicks for David Beckham. Both England goals came from free kicks when there had been no foul. England is a country of the gentleman, but I must say the referee was not acceptable." GREEK COACH, OTTO REHAGEL

"David Beckham virtually played Greece on his own." JOHN MOTSON

"It was David that won that match. He played like a true captain, and showed he really is the best player in the world. Right now, I love him." COMEDIAN FRANK SKINNER

"It looked like we were heading out of the competition, but we did it... thanks to David Beckham."

CHAT SHOW HOST MICHAEL PARKINSON

"David Beckham should be knighted. It was a great result and I'm still crying." SIR RICHARD BRANSON

"Beckham's performance was unique. Never before have I ever seen a player carry an entire team on his back at international level. Not Johan Cruyff, not Pele, not Maradona, not Zidane. He swept England up in his arms and carried them to the World Cup finals despite themselves. One day... the Queen will bestow the nation's highest honour upon one extremely proud subject: David Beckham. There is only one question... Why wait, Ma'am?**"**
JOHN SADLER, THE SUN

"I'm very proud to be Mrs. Beckham today..." VICTORIA

"I just couldn't have written a script like that. Captaining my country and scoring the goal at Old Trafford that took us through to the World Cup finals. That's fairytale stuff, isn't it?**"**

"Captain Golden Balls!" THE SUNDAY PEOPLE

"I've certainly lived up to my wife's nickname for me. I'm sure Victoria will be calling me 'Golden Balls'... tonight!**"**

Through The Keyhole

DAVID AND VICTORIA AIR THEIR VIEWS ON LIFE AT 'BECKINGHAM PALACE', HOME COOKING AND THE PRICE OF FAME...

"It's such a beautiful home. It took two years to finish and we're both so in love with it. The house has six bedrooms, and every room is themed. Our bedroom is very calm, with lots of white, and Brooklyn's room is amazing! I said to David, 'Can you believe it? We're 26 and 27 and we don't have a mortgage.' It's a big achievement."

"We've had a football pitch built at home for David and Brooklyn. It's actually a proper pitch, with underground watering. And do you know what they do? Put mummy in goal. Can you imagine? One gust of wind and I'm over!"

"I can sit there for hours and not say anything to David while being blissfully happy just watching television."

"For the first time in my life, I'm happy. I'm not Posh Spice to David and he's not a famous soccer star to me. We'd rather be cuddled up on the sofa watching *Blind Date* with a takeaway curry than out at a club."

"I'm not very domesticated. I can't really cook, so I do these ready-made meals that you just pierce at the top and stick in the oven for a couple of minutes. David, on the other hand, does everything. He cooks, he cleans, he's brilliant."

THROUGH THE KEYHOLE

“ David got that obsessive-compulsive thing where's everything's got to match. If you open our fridge, it's all co-ordinated. If there's only three cans of Diet Coke, he'll throw one away rather than have three – that's uneven. ”

“ David and I have these really loud checked pyjamas. I wear them and those big slippers with dogs on. The slippers are great, but if you don't walk right in them, you could trip downstairs and break your neck! ”

“ I'd rather live in a council flat with David than in 'Beckingham Palace' without him. ”

In May 2003, David and Victoria spent £1.5m on a holiday home in the South of France.

“ They have fallen in love with the South of France and have found the ideal spot to live. The house is set among woods and meadows and close to a natural spring. It is so romantic. Both David and Victoria are delighted with it. ”

A CLOSE FRIEND DESCRIBES THE DREAM HOME

"It's a challenge to play football against the best players in the world."

"At home, things can be hard. For instance, the curtains are never open. I get no privacy at all."

 "I liked Victoria for herself. I'd have liked her if she worked in Tesco."

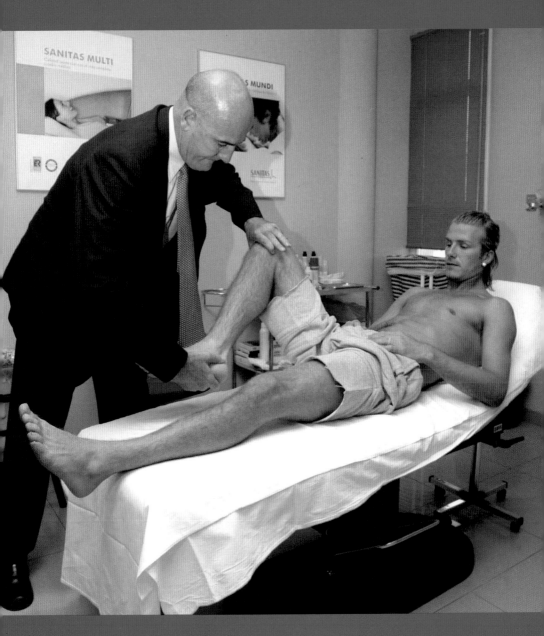

"**I dream a lot about football and a lot of them have come true for me.**"

The Price Of Fame...

"My first car cost £80,000. But my Dad didn't really like it. He's thinks it's nice, but not the sort of thing he'd go for. He'd get a big, comfortable... exactly!" DAVID

ON HOLIDAY IN DUBAI

"I can tell you exactly what I spend on food and petrol... and how much my car insurance costs. I do look at the price of things because I don't have the kind of money everyone thinks I do. I'm not going to pretend I'm skint, but I don't have £28 million! In fact, David never looks at the price of anything. It's the one thing he and I differ on. But I'm not going to be a nag bag. I'm here to make him happy."
VICTORIA

"People read in the papers about how much money I'm supposed to earn, where I live... where I go on holiday. They probably think 'Flash git'. But that's not how I see myself." DAVID

"David and I do a lot of stuff for charity. We're forever signing things, like football shirts and costumes, and auctioning them off. But we try to keep that side of our lives private." VICTORIA

"The dogs eat better than David and I do. They have dinner from Marks & Spencer every night... They wolf down about ten chickens. It's like feeding horses!" VICTORIA

THROUGH THE KEYHOLE

❝I don't really socialise a lot. If you add up the number of times David and I have been to premieres or launch parties, you could probably count it on one hand. We go out on Saturday night and we see our families. I've got a couple of really good friends but people do surprise you when they go to the newspapers and let you down – friends, people you've employed, ex-boyfriends... I do find it hard to trust people now.❞

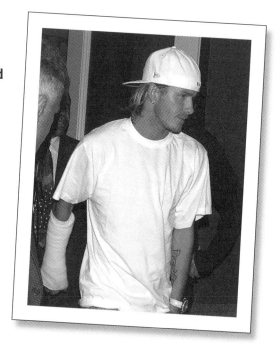

❝I've never actually been to Stringfellow's. I would never go somewhere like that.❞ DAVID

❝I don't go to clubs, so I don't meet many people. I'm wary of anyone. I think you've got to be.❞ DAVID

❝At home, things can be hard. For instance, the curtains are never open. I get no privacy at all. In fact, I can't remember the last time I saw daylight in my house.❞ DAVID

❝Victoria and I don't get that much time to spend with each other, so when we do, we tend to do *everything* together.❞ DAVID

❝Once those two step out of the door, it's an uphill battle for them to be able to do anything.❞ DANE BOWERS

"I'd love to wake up with David every morning and have dinner with him every night. And I'm sure that will happen one day. But, for the moment at least, we're both so busy. Still, being apart from each other makes it extra special when we are together."

"I long for us to be living together all the time. Sometimes I see a couple who've just finished work, sitting in their car and she's got her Barclays Bank badge on and he's got his Dixons badge on, and they're going home for dinner. Sometimes that looks so nice to me, but we all want something we don't have. I'm sure that couple go home and think, 'God, I wish we were like Posh and Becks. I wish we didn't have to worry about our mortgage'. David and I will be together every day one day though. Footballers retire at a relatively early age."

"Yes, I take my career and my family very seriously, but I'll also admit David and I are leading a really strange life. You've just got to have a sense of humour to go with it."

"People see me as miserable and up my own arse. They think I don't really care about anything but Prada and Gucci, that I boss David about and tell him what to wear. In most peoples' minds, I think I'm the Queen of England. And that is *so* not me. Bur people often believe what they read. I never complain about what's written about me, but if I read that stuff, I probably wouldn't like me either! When David and I look at 'Posh and Becks' in the papers, we think 'Bloody hate those two!'"

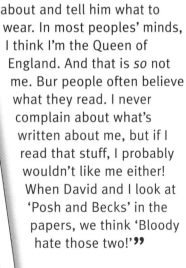

THROUGH THE KEYHOLE

Stars Rating

THE GREAT AND THE GOOD OFFER THEIR OPINIONS

"We are on David's case so much because he's such an young, outstanding footballer who has a pop star wife and a pop star life. He's constantly in the spotlight, but I think he courts it sometimes. Jamie Redknapp is married to Louise, but you don't see them in the papers every day. Victoria has her own TV programme on next week, and its all fantastic publicity for her... not for him. It's the Beckhams, front pages, middle pages and back pages!"

FOOTBALL PUNDIT MARK LAWRENSON

"David and Victoria deal with the attention they get tremendously well. I think they must have a very strong relationship to cope with it all. I've met Victoria at matches, and she's really friendly – a thoroughly nice girl. You know what? Sometimes, they leave themselves open to some criticism, but I'd never dream of giving (them) advice." POP STAR LOUISE NURDING AKA MRS. JAMIE REDKNAPP

"David's lifestyle, his marriage... he's very high profile. But there's never been a player who can cross the ball like him. Sometimes though, it's the other things that get more coverage."

FORMER ENGLAND MANAGER, KEVIN KEEGAN

"David's a really cool guy." TRUESTEPPER DANE BOWERS

"David Beckham's got a gift from God and he's using that gift."

PRINCE NASEEM

STARS RATING

"David Beckham is obviously the living God."

ANGUS DEAYTON

" Every boy wants to be in David's boots and every man wants to be in his missus. **"**

SACHA BARON COHEN AKA ALI G

"I'm very protective of David and Victoria. They're good friends of mine."

SIR ELTON JOHN

SACHA BARON COHEN AKA ALI G

" You don't get to be one of *the* great footballers... and manipulate the media anyway you choose without having a brain. What David does – and he does it very cleverly – is hide most of that brain from us all most of the time. That's pretty shrewd, actually... **"**

PIERS MORGAN, EDITOR OF THE DAILY MIRROR

**"It's impossible to be who he is, do what he's done and actually be stupid. I think people who believe that are just very naïve or just plain ignorant." ** DANE BOWERS

" You don't ever need to hear David Beckham speak. Just watch him play. That translates *globally*. **"** **RICHARD E. GRANT**

"And you must be the famous soccer star."

MADONNA MEETS DAVID FOR THE FIRST TIME

ALI G, INTERVIEWING, DAVID AND VICTORIA FOR CHILDREN IN NEED: " So, do you want Brooklyn to grow up to be a footballer like his dad, or a singer like Mariah Carey? **"**
VICTORIA: " I'm hoping he'll grow up to be a footballer like his dad, and that I'll grow up to be a singer like Mariah Carey. **"**

"The Ali G interview was hilarious. But when you get to know Victoria and David, you realise they are really funny and do have a great sense of humour. They don't mind taking the pee out of themselves." EMMA BUNTON

"I've met some of the biggest names in music, but David Beckham is the main man. He's a brilliant football player, and to meet him was a real honour.**"** R&B SUPERSTAR, USHER

"Posh and Becks? What would journalists do without them?"

SIMPLY RED'S MICK HUCKNALL

"Some woman asked me 'Are you so thin because you shag all day?' And I said 'Actually... yes. And I bet you would be too if you were married to David Beckham!'**"** VICTORIA REVEALS HER DIET SECRETS

"I look after myself. I eat well. I sleep well. It's important to look after your body. If you take care of yourself off the pitch, it sees you all right on the pitch."

"I'd pay £50,000 for a David Beckham interview. People are fascinated to find out what he eats for breakfast.**"** PIERS MORGAN

"David's surname's like a brand. I'm sure advertisers (think) ker-ching!" RICHARD E. GRANT

"I am so not sporty in every way. Give me a tennis racket and I wouldn't know which end to use. I stand in goal and David and Brooklyn just kick footballs at me!**"**

VICTORIA DESCRIBES FILLING IN FOR FABIAN BARTHEZ

RICHARD E. GRANT

STARS RATING

"David Beckham is a hugely important figure in popular culture and probably now the most influential male figure for anyone in Britain aged five to 60...he has broken so many strict, traditional working-class masculine codes of behaviour that he has the potential to influence lots of boys and young men to do the same; for example, accepting homosexuality as part of life. We hope a spin-off will be to make the world a better, more tolerant place.**"** DR. ANDREW PARKER OF WARWICK UNIVERSITY

In January 2003, news of the latest Pepsi commercial was unveiled. It starred David and a host of United stars in a spoof spaghetti Western, for which they were flown to Almeria in Spain.

"A lot of them were incredible actors but Beckham was just great.**"**
DIRECTOR TARSEM SINGH

"I used to play cowboys and Indians as a boy. I was always the cowboy, though.**"** DAVID

"I walk into a bar and the Real keeper Casillas drinks my Pepsi. So I take him outside for a penalty shoot-out and it goes on from there.**"** DAVID REVEALS THE PLOT

Also in January, David was immortalised in oils when a controversial painting bearing his image as a Christ-like figure is unveiled at a gallery in Fulham, West London.

The work is entitled "Goldenballs", which copies a pet name that Victoria had used in the past.

❝I see David Beckham as a modern-day religious icon, a person who appears as a god.❞ **ARTIST SHARON LUTCHMAN**

In June 2003, David and Victoria had heads turning when they stole the show at the MTV Movie Awards in Hollywood:

❝He's the best footballer in the world and she's really beautiful.❞

SAMUEL L. JACKSON

❝**The guy's my hero. I think he's absolutely gorgeous. Everyone is smitten with Becks and Posh.**❞ BEYONCE

❝They're a nice couple and he's so talented.❞ **HARRISON FORD**

❝**He's an amazingly talented guy. She's very beautiful.**❞

GEORGE LUCAS

❝That was the most phenomenal entrance I have ever seen. They are sooooo Hollywood, so glam and over the top. They are the new Ben Affleck and J-Lo. They were just so amazing – totally tasteless but glam and so bling, bling, bling.❞

STEVEN COJOCARU, PEOPLE MAGAZINE

STARS RATING

You Wear It Well...

DAVID ON FASHION... VICTORIA ON NOT DRESSING DAVID

"There's been a lot of rubbish bandied around about Victoria not liking the city – not liking the shops or whatever. It's just a load of nonsense. She likes Manchester. Victoria is happy wherever I am happy and that's it." **DAVID**

"I do really love Manchester. There's been a lot of rumours that I don't, but I do. And David's very happy there. Anyway, he wouldn't look very good in a blue shirt, would he?"

"If Victoria wears a certain pair of shoes or a certain dress, you can bet they'll be a little girl... saying to her mum, 'That's the dress I want'. But as Victoria says, we've never set ourselves up to be idolised." **DAVID**

David and a host of others talk about his contribution to British fashion...

"Who would ever have believed that the fashion industry would consider Eminem to be more powerful than Ralph Lauren, or David Beckham to have more influence than Giorgio Armani?"
LOADED FASHION EDITOR/STYLE GURU ADRIAN CLARK

"David Beckham is one of the few men other men talk about being dead-on handsome." RICHARD E. GRANT

YOU WEAR IT WELL...

"Sometimes I do wonder what I look like. Do I look OK? Have I got a double chin?" **DAVID**

"David's so famous now – but not just through his football. If you didn't know him through that, you'd certainly know him through his wife who dresses him funny." ULRIKA JOHNSON

"David knows a lot about clothes, and we both help each other out. If I go shopping and I see something that will look good on him, I'll buy it for him. He does the same thing for me. He's very good at picking stuff. It's a shame he's so busy, because he'd make a great stylist."

"We've got matching dogs, matching watches, matching Jaguars and similar clothes. I like that. Yes, I know it's tacky, but it makes me laugh."

"If I want convince David to do something, I just make him think it was his idea."

"Victoria obviously talked him into wearing that sarong."

VICTORIA'S STYLIST, KENNY HO

"A lot of people ask me about that, but I can't take the credit..."

VICTORIA ON THE SARONG

"It doesn't mean a guy is gay because he wears a skirt. Men can look very masculine in skirts – sexy and cheeky."

RAP SUPERSTAR PI DIDDY/ PUFF DADDY

❝I've had a certain amount of abuse in my life... look at the sarong. To be honest, it just goes completely over my head.❞ **DAVID**

❝**I always tell him he looks lovely.**❞ VICTORIA

❝Three lions & a skirt.❞
THE SUN

❝**I don't really care whether he wears a sarong, has a mohican haircut or just walks around in his underpants.**❞
GARY LINEKER

❝David comes up with his own hairstyles. Honestly, I have nothing to do with them.❞ **VICTORIA**

❝**My haircut didn't cost £300. A mate did it for me... I just fancied a change.**❞ DAVID

❝You know what? David can wear anything... do anything with his hair and he still looks great. He's just naturally good-looking and talented... it's sickening!❞ **VICTORIA**

❝**David wears my knickers. He's getting in touch with his feminine side.**❞ VICTORIA, 1998

❝Of course he doesn't wear my knickers. I was joking... He couldn't fit one of his legs in my knickers, for God's sake!❞
VICTORIA, 2001

YOU WEAR IT WELL...

HELENA CHRISTENSEN MODELLING
A PHILIP TREACY DESIGNED 'DAVID BECKHAM HAT' AT THE
BROWN THOMAS INTERNATIONAL FASHION SHOW, DUBLIN

"We're portrayed as very different people to the ones we actually are. And Victoria says things now and again that make it a little worse for me... like the knicker incident. No, I don't wear her knickers. She's a little smaller than me."

"I call David 'Golden Balls'. Oops, that's one of those things I shouldn't have said, isn't it?"

"I always say 'For God's sake, Victoria!' She just doesn't listen..."

"You looked really nice on the pitch. Your hair needs doing though – your roots are coming through."

VICTORIA OFFERS DAVID CRITICAL ADVICE DURING WORLD CUP '98

"I've got a big mouth, haven't I? I suppose I just like talking!"

VICTORIA

"David's one eyebrow short of a face, isn't he?" ULRIKA JOHNSON

"The eyebrow shaving was just a fad I went through. Usually, you go through that stage at sixteen or seventeen. I'm still going through it at the age of twenty six! I didn't do it for the publicity though..."

"(Shaving his eyebrow) made him more aerodynamic!"

VICTORIA

❝The areas of success that we have achieved so far in David Beckham DB07 and schoolwear gives us an indication of what we need to do to build a better recovery.❞

MARKS & SPENCER'S CHIEF EXECUTIVE ROGER HOLMES DEMONSTRATES
THE IMPORTANCE OF DAVID'S BRANDED CLOTHING

❝Obviously, there's a slight conflict because Victoria wants to be on the front pages and David probably doesn't. But that's something they've learned to live with.❞ **GARY LINEKER**

❝There are times when they kick each other's butts a bit, sure. Victoria's a very strong-minded person, and I certainly wouldn't want to get into an argument with her. David's a good lad for putting up with her... yes, indeed.❞ DANE BOWERS

❝It must be hard sometimes... having such a famous wife.❞

MICHAEL OWEN

YOU WEAR IT WELL... ❞

Just The Two Of Us

DAVID AND VICTORIA ON LOVE AND LIFE TOGETHER

"I want people to look back at me and not remember the front pages, but instead say 'He was a player.'**"** DAVID

"What I'd really like to do at the end of my career is to open a school of excellence for kids, boys and girls. I know it's not a normal ambition for a footballer, but it's something I've always wanted to do. A lot of people helped me get to where I am and I want to put something tangible back into the game." DAVID

" David's a very private person, a very intelligent person. And he makes me laugh. Yet, People say such terrible things about him... that he's thick. That he hasn't got a brain... that I boss him about. But he's such a strong character. In our house, I'd say he's the dominant one. "

VICTORIA

" **My whole life took on a new meaning with the birth of our first son Brooklyn. It was a fantastic experience and taught me what real happiness is all about. I also have much to be thankful for in my professional and private life. I am with the woman I love, and we have a beautiful child. I play for the greatest football club in the world and have been blessed with the talent which enables me to play for my country.** "

" There are so many good things in my life, the black moments never last long. All the criticism can just fly over my head as long as I've got Victoria to come home to. "

" **This is the first time I've been in love. I think once you meet the person that you want to spend the rest of your life with, you know. And no matter what is going on around you, you dedicate your life to that person – you never hurt or destroy that relationship.** " DAVID

" A lot of people would love to see David and I split up, without a doubt. But there's a trust between us, and as long as that's there, then it will always be the relationship it is. "

" **The hardest part of my life is when I'm away from David. Everything else I can cope with.** "

" Since I've got to know Victoria, I just love her more and more... she's the only woman I've ever loved. "

JUST THE TWO OF US 99

Where's Your Metatarsal?

ON 10 APRIL 2002, DAVID BECKHAM BROKE THE SECOND METATARSAL BONE IN HIS LEFT FOOT WHILE PLAYING FOR MANCHESTER UNITED IN A 3-2 WIN OVER DEPORTIVO LA CORUNA IN THE CHAMPIONS LEAGUE

The injury cast doubt over Beckham's chances of leading England into the World Cup:

"When I stood up, I knew I'd broken something. The first question I asked the surgeon was if I was out of the World Cup. I was devastated."

"David called me from the hospital to let me know how he was. To be honest, he was devastated. He's very, very upset, in plaster and in a lot of pain. He said he was more upset because of the games coming up. I feel sorry for him. It's a terrible thing to have happened, but fingers crossed, he'll be OK..."

TED BECKHAM, DAVID'S FATHER

"This is a real blow for David personally, for Manchester United and for England, but there is nothing we can do about it. I am sure, however, that the medical staff at Manchester United will do everything in their power to ensure David recovers fully and quickly." SVEN-GORAN ERIKSSON

"Managers can name a replacement for an injured player up to 24 hours before the tournament starts. Therefore, Sven-Goran Eriksson has until 30 May to decide whether to include David Beckham in his final 23-man England squad." FIFA REPRESENTATIVE

WHERE'S YOUR METATARSAL?

"The prognosis is slightly better. Clearly, with an injury of this type, the first 48 hours are crucial, but things do sound a little better. Hopefully, David's foot will improve."

FA CHIEF EXECUTIVE ALAN CROZIER

"David is young. He'll play in other matches." SIR ALEX FERGUSON

"Let's not forget, David's unbelievably fit. And he's a quick healer."

ERIC HARRISON, MANCHESTER UNITED COACH

"I didn't like the oxygen tent. I tried it out, but I just couldn't sleep in it. They say you have to spend eight hours in it – I couldn't spend eight minutes in it! I hate the thing. It might work for some people but not for me." DAVID DISSES THE OXYGEN TANK "CURE"

"I'm not a miracle worker but if millions of people focus their mind on David's foot, we can unleash a powerful healing force. I want people to touch their TV screens. Take it seriously – if just for a few seconds – send David some healing energy."

URI GELLER BEAMS HEALTH RAYS TO DAVID'S FOOT VIA GMTV

"The Prime Minister has pointed out that nothing is more important to England's arrangements for the World Cup than the state of David Beckham's left foot."

SPOKESMAN FOR THE PRIME MINISTER

"I've had a lot of offers of treatment from all over the world. I've also had a lot of letters of support and really have to thank my fans. Also, the people at Manchester United have been great with me – every minute of the day, using things like laser treatment."

DAVID PAYS TRIBUTE TO HIS SUPPORT NETWORK

"I have come to accept that if I have a new haircut it is front-page news but having a picture of my foot on the front page of a national newspaper is a bit exceptional."

"With Ronaldo and Zidane, David Beckham is one of the biggest superstars in the world. If he doesn't come to Japan and South Korea, it will hurt the World Cup."

YOSHIHKO KONNO, SPORTS EDITOR, DAILY SPORT

"It's difficult when David wants to be out there playing and he can't. It's just very frustrating for him...hobbling around the house, but it's not easy for me either. Obviously Brooklyn needs a lot of attention and with me being heavily pregnant, it's hard for me to pick him up – Brooklyn's really heavy. But we're coping. It's just nice to have David home." VICTORIA

"Victoria's been unbelievable. Six months pregnant and she's getting me cups of tea. I've been on crutches for three weeks and she's been carrying everything, including Brooklyn. It's been hard work for her but she's been amazing."

"My foot's still a bit sore but I'm going to get fit. It shouldn't be much of a problem. After all, there are still three weeks left to the start of the World Cup..."

"Don't worry. David will be fit. He's done all the training. I think he has sufficient time – there's no big rush. He's a naturally fit athlete and it's not a big mountain for him to climb. It's within David's capacity to lift himself. After all, he's a player who likes the big stage – he thrives on it." **SIR ALEX FERGUSON**

"David is ready. England are ready. Let's see..."
SVEN-GORAN ERIKSSON

WHERE'S YOUR METATARSAL?

Big In Japan

THE 2002 WORLD CUP FINALS

"Win the World Cup David and You Can Have the Job"
DAILY MIRROR HEADLINE OFFERS DAVID THE JOB OF PRIME MINISTER.

"I want to be the new Bobby Moore. I know I'm following in the footsteps of England captains like him. Bobby Moore walked into a room and people stood up and clapped. He was a gentleman and a great captain. That's always stuck in my mind."

"David will be able to compete in our first World Cup game against Sweden. We've assessed him – free kicks, shooting and lots and lots of running. Until last week, we didn't know who to play on the right. We had options but not another Beckham. But now I'm confident he'll be able to withstand tackles. I'm very optimistic."
SVEN-GORAN ERIKSSSON

"I want to make an impression at this World Cup. I've worked harder over the last seven weeks than I ever have to be fit. All the players are ready and I'm confident we can do well."

"I have a feeling my time has come."
DAVID'S REACTION ON TRYING HIS NEW ADIDAS 'NINJA' FOOTBALL BOOTS

"My left foot feels a lot better, thanks. When you break a bone, you don't know what's going to happen, but I always had it in my mind I'd be fit for the Swedish game. I'm confident I can last the full 90 minutes. It wouldn't be fair to the rest of the squad if I wasn't sure."

BIG IN JAPAN

"It's amazing when 20 people chase our coach chanting 'David' or 'Michael'. But our focus has to remain on the players, the staff and the Sweden game. We honestly believe we can beat them and go on from there."

"There's no point going into the World Cup thinking you're going to draw or get beaten. We want to go as far as we can. We're not out here for a laugh or a joke. This is the 'Group of Death' and we're in it."

Sunday, 3 June 2002
England 1 Sweden 1

"Same old story for Sven's Men" DAILY EXPRESS HEADLINE

"If we play like that again, we'll definitely be in trouble. We just can't afford to sit back. For me, after two months out, and in the humidity, I was a bit tired. To be honest, my legs disappeared in the second half. That's never happened to me before."

"We're disappointed we didn't beat Sweden, but I'm pleased we're going to face Argentina. I'm very proud to be leading my country out against them. For us, it doesn't get much bigger than Argentina – unless it's the World Cup Final itself."

"England's results against Argentina in the past have not been good but that's in the past."

"I know a little bit of the story between England and Argentina. But if you go into the match in a sporting way, with a great desire to win, that's a positive thing. But if you look for revenge and feel only hate, that's very dangerous...This is the game to find out about the young players. Hopefully, David can last the full 90 minutes. Of course, he is our captain and we expect a lot of him in such a big game. But we'll just have to wait and see..."

SVEN-GORAN ERIKSSON

Friday, 7 June 2002
England 1 Argentina 0

"Up Yours Senors!**"** FRONT PAGE HEADLINE, THE SUN

"It doesn't get any sweeter than this. It's definitely the most satisfying goal I've scored in my life."

DAVID ON HIS MATCH-WINNING PENALTY

"I just wanted to put the ghost to rest after my World Cup got turned upside down four years ago. I don't usually get nervous taking penalties but this time I was. I just ran up and hit it as hard as I could. I caught it cleanly and was just so happy it went in.**"**

"Actually, Sir Alex rang me the night before the game and said "Good Luck, enjoy it and pace yourself." And I did."

"The team showed such courage, such bravery. I might have scored the penalty, but from David Seaman in goal all the way up to the front two, the whole side was magnificent.**"**

BIG IN JAPAN

"Nigeria look strong and have players capable of hurting us. Of course, we're still on a high after the Argentina match, but we have to get our attitude right. To slip up now would be ridiculous."

After a goalless draw against Nigeria, England faced Denmark in the second phase...

Saturday, 16 June 2002
England 3 Denmark 0

"Goldane Balls!" FRONT PAGE HEADLINE, SUNDAY PEOPLE

"England played well but I'm especially proud of David. We spoke before the game and he said he felt really fit and up for it. He didn't score today but he was still a brilliant captain. It's just a shame [because of the pregnancy] I can't be there to see it in person." VICTORIA

"It's a shame Victoria couldn't come. But she's seven-and-a-half months pregnant and it might be dangerous for her. Anyway, she doesn't mind me kissing the goalscorers. As long as they're boys, she won't be bothered."

"I'm so proud of the team. They're not afraid to play real football. They're all heroes."

"We don't care who we come up against... now bring on Brazil."

Friday, 21 June 2002
England 1 Brazil 2

❝Anyone for Tennis?**❞ FRONT-PAGE HEADLINE, DAILY MIRROR**

❝You worked hard out there. You did a good job. It's not your fault he fluked it, is it? Eh? Eh?❞ DAVID CONSOLES GOALKEEPER DAVID SEAMAN
AFTER RONALDINHO'S FREAK GOAL SENT ENGLAND OUT OF THE WORLD CUP FINALS

❝I just want to say sorry to the rest of the lads and the people back home. It was a fluke goal. Sometimes, that's just the way it goes.**❞**
CAPTAIN DAVID KEEPS A STIFF UPPER LIP

❝We could have won this tournament. We were close but not close enough. I hoped we could do a little better. It's a pity but I have no regrets...I'm staying put and so is my team. We'll be back for World Cup 2006 – wiser and stronger. I'm just proud to be England manager.❞ SVEN-GORAN ERIKSSON

❝To reach the Quarter Finals with a team full of players in their first World Cup is some achievement. We should be proud of ourselves for reaching this point. I had a funny feeling we were going to go

all the way but it wasn't meant to be. But we have to thank our fans for sticking with us and Japan and South Korea – the way they supported us was amazing. I'd rather be staying on than going home but it's been a fantastic experience for us all. I think the England team will come back all the better for what we've been through here. And remember, there's always a next time.**❞**

❝They're all heroes❞
VICTORIA

BIG IN JAPAN

Act Two: Enter Romeo

THE EXCITEMENT MOUNTED THROUGH THE SUMMER OF 2002 AS DAVID AND VICTORIA PREPARED TO BE PARENTS FOR A SECOND TIME

"Victoria and I really wanted to have another baby. It was just another case of picking when to have one because we're always so busy."

"Anyone who's ever had kids knows the moment you have one – whether it's a son or a daughter – it's the best feeling in the world."

"Brooklyn's a very affectionate little boy so he's going to be brilliant with the new baby. He's running about – kicking footballs, singing, dancing. He's a big boy now."

"Brooklyn was the first person I told when the doctor confirmed I was pregnant. Then I sent him over to tell David the secret. David was practically in tears, he was so happy." VICTORIA

"I can't for the new baby to be born" SANDRA BECKHAM, DAVID'S MOTHER

VICTORIA: **"I love being pregnant. I like giving birth. Actually, I love it."**
DAVID: **"Victoria, you had a caesarean. You didn't even feel it!"**

"Overall, this has been a very exciting year for us. England are in the World Cup finals, Victoria's had her second Top Ten hit and now, we're expecting a new baby. It's fantastic."

ACT TWO: ENTER ROMEO

The Birth

On Sunday, 1 September 2002, Victoria gave birth to a 7lb 4oz baby boy, Romeo, at Portland Hospital.

"Romeo's gorgeous and Victoria's great. She's just sitting up in bed and all the family are here. The name? Romeo's just a name we love. We're both delighted."

"Yes, it's an unusual name. In that way, it's the same as Brooklyn. But it's David and Victoria's choice, so it's obviously what they wanted. But I know if Romeo turns out to be half as good as Brooklyn, he will be wonderful. I'm over the moon."

TED BECKHAM, DAVID'S FATHER

"Romeo looks just like Brooklyn. He's got his nose and Victoria's chin. I was there when Romeo came out. It was awesome. Victoria and I might try and work on a five-a-side team in the next few months!"

"With David and I coaching, we'll have a good little side there..." TED BECKHAM

"Brooklyn came in just as Romeo was coming out. He's in awe of him."

"You're always nervous having children but it's still the most beautiful thing in the world. Victoria is delighted."

"We had a number of people asking for a price but it was just too near the birth so we had the sense to turn them all down, so we're quite happy and we will start laying bets at 250-1 that Romeo will play for England."

GRAHAM SHARPE OF BOOKMAKERS WILLIAM HILL EXPLAINS HOW PUNTERS TRIED TO BET ON THE NAME ROMEO

"I don't think Romeo's named after me, but if he is, I'm overwhelmed. I'd also like to wish the Beckhams 'congratulations'. Nice choice of name, definitely. Actually, I reckon little Romeo will be a hit with the ladies with a name like that. Big up the Beckhams."

MC ROMEO, SO SOLID CREW

ACT TWO: ENTER ROMEO

From Manchester To Madrid

ON 15TH FEBRUARY 2003, DAVID EMERGED FROM OLD TRAFFORD SPORTING STICHES IN A CUT ABOVE THE EYEBROW. AMAZINGLY, THE INJURY WAS UNWITTINGLY INFLICTED BY A FLYING BOOT KICKED BY SIR ALEX FERGUSON, ENRAGED BY UNITED'S DEFEAT TO ARSENAL IN AN FA CUP TIE

"If there is no apology there is no telling where this could go"

A CLOSE FRIEND BRIEFS THE PRESS

"Whatever happens in the dressing room remains private"

A UNITED SPOKESMAN REVEALS MUCH IN GIVING AWAY NOTHING

"David did not want stitches at first, but two hours after the game blood was still dripping from the wound and the club doctor visited David's house and fixed two steri-strips to stop the bleeding"

STATEMENT FROM DAVID'S MANAGEMENT COMPANY

"I want to assure all Manchester United fans that there is complete harmony and focus as we prepare for the Juventus game. The dressing room incident was just one of those things, it's all in the past now." DAVID GIVES THE SUBJECT THE BOOT

"It upset David, he didn't want that. He rang me afterwards and he wasn't happy but he didn't deliberately get photographed. He just went out shopping. He had a cut eyebrow. What could he have worn to cover it – sunglasses, a massive hat, a balaclava? It was ridiculous. If he is in the paper every day I understand the manager getting wound up and it created a problem between them publicly, definitely."

TED BECKHAM, DAVID'S FATHER

"The publicity it created? The only reaction I have to that is that it was a freakish incident. If I tried it a hundred or a million times it couldn't happen again. If it did I would have carried on playing...it was a graze that was dealt with by the doctor. There is no problem and we move on." ALEX FERGUSON BREAKS HIS SILENCE

"I've got a stack of football boots here under the table."

TONY BLAIR JOKES WITH JOURNALISTS BEFORE A PRESS CONFERENCE

Within weeks, the transfer rumour mill was at full tilt.

"If we want to buy a player, we talk to the club first and ask if the player is available. Manchester United would know first and they don't know a thing about it, so there is nothing true about it."

ARSENAL MANAGER ARSENE WENGER RULES OUT THE GUNNERS, 19TH FEBRUARY

"I've lived in Manchester for about twelve years now but I'll always be a Londoner, no-one is going to change that. There is a possibility that I could play for a London club one day. You never say never in football because things can change so quickly, so I wouldn't rule it out." DAVID KEEPS THEM GUESSING

"I have heard a lot about this recently but I don't want to raise hopes about signing Beckham and then see he can't come here. He is a great player but we will not sign everyone on the market.**"**

REAL MADRID'S PRESIDENT, FLORENTINO PEREZ, 18TH MARCH

"I've always said that Real Madrid have some great players and great traditions. Any player would be honoured to be spoken about by Real Madrid. So, of course, I'm honoured."

DAVID, 26TH MARCH

"There are always going to be certain rumours flying about and I'm used to that now...I just get on with my football and don't worry about anything else going on or being said about me.**"**

DAVID, 26TH MARCH

"The possibility he will one day play for Real Madrid is very remote" REAL MADRID SPORTING DIRECTOR JORE VALDANO ON A POSSIBLE BECKHAM MOVE, 27TH MARCH

"Madrid have some great players and if the coach wants to introduce a player such as Beckham into the team and the team is triumphant, then that's great."

1950S REAL MADRID LEGEND ALFREDO DI STEFANO

"The way Real Madrid have pulled off the biggest transfer market coups of the last few seasons, Beckham looks like the next big transfer project for us.**"**

VALDANO HAS A RAPID CHANGE OF HEART, 31ST MARCH

FROM MANCHESTER TO MADRID

"I don't know if Inter [Milan] really want Beckham. As far as we are concerned, Inter have the green light for Beckham because we are not going to enter any auction."

VALDANO AGAIN, 4TH APRIL

"If the president thinks it is important for us, it is okay with me but I don't think it is necessary for the team... if he does come, I will not be worried." **REAL'S MIDFIELD MAESTRO LUIS FIGO**

"It is totally out of the question. There is no way we would sell him or any of our best players." SIR ALEX FERGUSON

8th April. David is left out of United's biggest game of the season, the Champions League quarter-final against Real Madrid. Appearing belatedly as a sub, he scores but United still go out.

"This could be it for him now. He is extremely unhappy about being left out." **A CLOSE FRIEND DOES THE TALKING**

"When I asked him if he was going to move, he started asking me questions about the quality of primary schools in Madrid."

RICARDO, REAL'S GOALKEEPER, REVEALS A POST-MATCH CONVERSATION WITH DAVID

"I greeted him affectionately after the game on Wednesday night. I don't know if he is coming to Madrid or not but I am certain it won't be difficult to find a place for him."

MADRID'S BRAZILIAN STAR RONALDO

"I don't think he wants to go anywhere. He loves it at United, that's where his heart is. On Wednesday after the game he told me he was disappointed, devastated really, about not being chosen for the game. I think he should have played but I would say that, being his dad." TED BECKHAM

❝ I always get asked whether David Beckham is a good player. Of course he's a good player and, of course, the club would want him, but I also get asked what schools he would send his children to and where would he live? I haven't got a clue, no-one has told me anything. Our season doesn't finish until June 22nd. If something happens, then it would probably happen after that. **❞**

REAL MADRID AND EX-LIVERPOOL WINGER STEVE MCMANAMAN, 24TH APRIL

DAVID TRAINING WITH STEVE McMANAMAN

❝ When Madrid come for you they make it almost impossible to turn them down and David Beckham would find himself in a similar position. ❞

MADRID'S FRENCH ACE ZINEDINE ZIDANE

ZINEDINE ZIDANE

❝ As I've always said, never say never. You always want to play with the best team and the best players. Undoubtedly, Manchester United have a great team and great players. In the last eight, nine years we've won most things in England and the European Cup. Real Madrid have got a massive history about them and they've got world-class players. **❞**

DAVID, 29TH APRIL

FROM MANCHESTER TO MADRID **❞❞**

BECKS *Talking*

"Surrounding the speculation regarding the supposed interest from Real Madrid in signing David Beckham, the club wishes to communicate that:

"No contact has existed between Real Madrid and Manchester United on this issue.

"Neither directly or indirectly has there been any contact between Real Madrid and Mr Beckham.

"Despite the speculation surrounding this issue, Madrid have no intention of negotiating the transfer of Mr. Beckham.

"Against the general policy of the club which never uses official sources to reject rumours, this press release has been issued with the objective of putting an end to the growing speculation which has circulated without any foundation linking Mr. Beckham with Real Madrid.

"On top of the recent rumours, the unconditional friendly relationship between both clubs and the respect due for Mr. Beckham still remains." OFFICIAL REAL MADRID STATEMENT, 29TH APRIL

"Never, never, never. Nobody at Real Madrid has ever spoken about Beckham and I do not want to say more about this matter myself."
REAL MADRID'S PRESIDENT FLORENTINO PEREZ WHEN FIRST ASKED
ABOUT THE POSSIBLE ARRIVAL OF DAVID BECKHAM, 30TH APRIL

"I am delighted Mr Perez has confirmed this in such an emphatic manner but, anyway, we at Manchester United never had any intention of selling him." UNITED CHIEF EXECUTIVE PETER KENYON

"There's been a lot of stuff in the media about me and my future but I can honestly say that there has been no contact between either me or my adviser, with Real Madrid, or any other club. My feelings for Manchester United, the club itself, the players, the fans and the backroom staff, are as strong as ever."
DAVID BREAKS HIS SILENCE, 6TH MAY

"I know Peter Kenyon and the manager are saying they want me to stay and that's good enough for me. My affection for the club has never changed from the day I signed for United." 6TH MAY

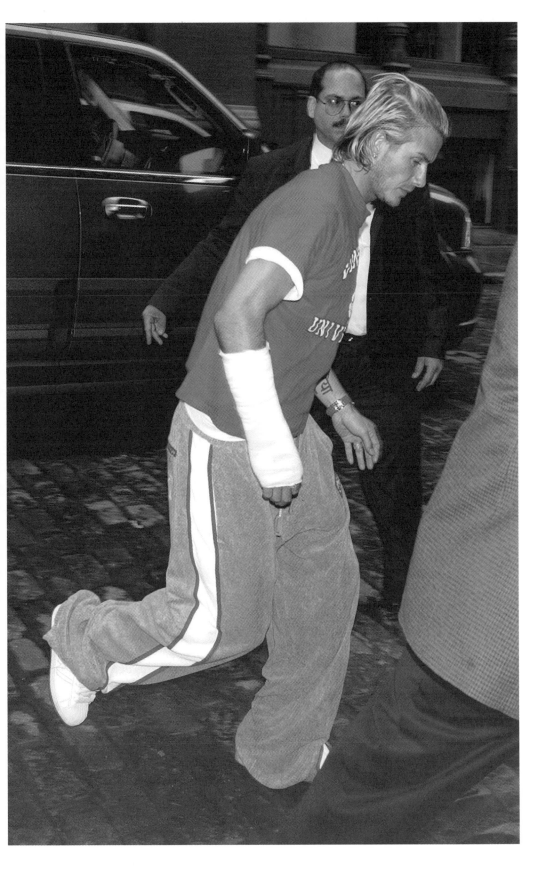

❝Given [the story] has come out of Spain, I don't think you would look stupid writing it.❞

KENYON HAS A CHANGE OF HEART, 7 MAY

❝David Beckham is the one soccer player that most people in the States would instantly recognise. It's more to do with the fact that he is married to a former Spice Girl than his prowess on the field but that is almost immaterial. Among the soccer-loving public here, Beckham is on a par with Ronaldo so, while we have to remember that it's Manchester United who are being promoted to play here, it is great news that he will be coming.❞

CHARLIE STILLITANO, CHIEF EXECUTIVE OF US SPORTS PROMOTERS
CHAMPIONSWORLD, ON UNITED'S SUMMER TOUR

❝I haven't been contacted, my agent hasn't been contacted and neither has Manchester United. I want to stay at Manchester United.❞ **7TH MAY**

❝There have been talks.❞

ITV'S DES LYNAM CLAIMS TO HAVE READ DAVID'S LIPS AFTER UNITED'S
FINAL GAME OF THE SEASON, 11TH MAY

66You don't spend twelve months negotiating a new contract to give up on it twelve months later. We re-signed David because we saw him as part of our squad for the next three years.**99**

PETER KENYON, 7TH MAY

66David is a critical part of our squad but things change... even if David sees out the rest of his career at United there will be a time when we have to replace him.99 PETER KENYON, 11TH MAY

66Couldn't you see that by the way he celebrated winning the Championship trophy last weekend? Didn't that tell you how much he wanted to stay? There is so much stuff written about him, the majority of it is wrong.**99** TED BECKHAM, DAVID'S FATHER, 18TH MAY

66Beckham is a great man, a great player. He can play at Inter Milan or at Real Madrid but if I was Manchester United I would never let him leave. He knows how to play football like no-one else.99 ENGLAND COACH SVEN-GORAN ERIKSSON, 24TH MAY

66As for hopes, well I have mine too – I want Sensi to buy Beckham.**99**   AS ROMA BOSS FABIO CAPPELLO OFFERS SOME ADVICE FOR HIS CLUB'S PRESIDENT FRANCO SENSI, 31ST MAY

66I view this [£30m] as a great price for Beckham. He is one of the few players in the world capable of earning the money back for you in commercial revenue alone.99

JOAN LAPORTA, CANDIDATE FOR PRESIDENCY OF BARCELONA, 1ST JUNE

66It would be impossible for us to move him for such a high figure.**99**

MILAN'S VICE-PRESIDENT ADRIANO GALLIANI BAULKS AT THE PROSPECT OF A £35M FEE, 1ST JUNE

66He has said that he wants to stay there. If the club alter their view, and it needs all parties to change their view, then, of course, everything is possible in football.99

SFX SPORTS, DAVID'S MANAGEMENT COMPANY

FROM MANCHESTER TO MADRID

❝Our conversations with Manchester United are very advanced and progressing very well. We will also talk to David and his agent. That is how it is always done. We will not confirm any deals until it is done. He will be the leader of the team, the Cruyff of 1973 for FC Barcelona.❞

JOAN LAPORTA

❝**Manchester United can confirm that clubs from Italy and Spain have expressed a firm interest in signing David Beckham. David's advisers, SFX, have also been approached by clubs independently and we are in regular and close contact with them regarding the status of those discussions, which are ongoing. David has been kept informed while on holiday.**❞ STATEMENT FROM MANCHESTER UNITED, 7TH JUNE

❝ These rumours have been going on for about two months now. About a month ago, it was Real Madrid and now it's Barcelona. But I'm a Man. United player. As long as they want me, I'll stay. But I've never said I'd never move away from Manchester.❞

DAVID SPEAKING ON 10TH JUNE

❝**I'd rather jack it in than leave United. They're the only team I've ever wanted to play for. I'm absolutely gutted over what's happened.**❞

❝United have always been my first club and I've had so many years with some of the world 's quality players at Old Trafford. I don't want to go anywhere and the club confirming talks with Barcelona has left me speechless.❞

"If the club don't want me that's something beyond my control but my heart is at Old Trafford and I can't believe the way things have snowballed while I've been away."

"Manchester United confirms that in the event of all of the conditions are fulfilled then the offer would be acceptable.**"**

CLUB STATEMENT CONFIRMS UNITED'S CONSIDERATION OF A BID
FROM BARCELONA, 10TH JUNE

"David is very surprised and disappointed to learn of this statement and has no plans to meet to Mr Laporta or his representatives."

DAVID'S MANAGEMENT COMPANY SFX REACT TO UNITED'S STATEMENT

"I've never said that I'd never move away from Manchester and I've never said that I'd end my career there. With all the big teams there are always going to be changes, because you look to strengthen the team whether you win three trophies or you win one.**"**

FINALLY, DAVID APPEARS TO HAVE A CHANGE OF HEART, 10TH JUNE

"I don't want him to go. I shall tell him not to go there [Barcelona]. I shall tell him to stay at Manchester United."

TED BECKHAM

"What a way to treat an England hero!**"**

DAILY MIRROR HEADLINE
SLAMS UNITED FOR THEIR
TREATMENT OF DAVID

FROM MANCHESTER TO MADRID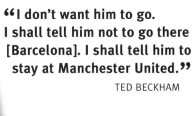

Meanwhile, On The Pitch...

DURING THE WEEKS OF SPECULATION, DAVID WAS STILL IN THE THICK OF THE FOOTBALLING ACTION FOR MANCHESTER UNITED AND, IN PARTICULAR, FOR ENGLAND, WHOSE FIRST TASK WAS TO PREPARE FOR A FRIENDLY INTERNATIONAL AGAINST AUSTRALIA

> **"**I'm sure that David will look after Wayne Rooney, he does that sort of thing very well. I don't think I even need to ask David, he will just do it naturally. He does that all the time when young players come in and is very, very good as a captain.**"**
>
> **ENGLAND COACH SVEN-GORAN ERIKSSON**

Wednesday, 12th February 2003
England 1 Australia 3

David plays the first half only as the entire team, in a pre-arranged tactic, are substituted at half-time. England's defeat is their first against the Aussies.

MEANWHILE, ON THE PITCH...

“We are very disappointed. The eleven who came off would have loved to have stayed on and that's the disappointing and annoying thing about playing half a game, but the manager had no choice in the matter. The club-versus-country thing has been a big issue all week and was sort of topped off with the way things went on the night.”

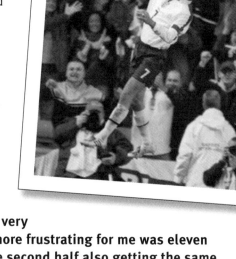

“We didn't give the young lads a chance in the second half. We got booed off at half time, which is not much fun and very frustrating but what was more frustrating for me was eleven young lads out there in the second half also getting the same treatment. They certainly didn't deserve that.”

“That for me was more disappointing than having a go at the senior players, who can accept that to a certain extent. Maybe it wasn't directed at them. Maybe it was directed towards the first-half performance but for many of the young lads it was their first game, which they are going to remember for a long time. I don't think it will damage them and I'm not sure if they noticed it as much as I did, but I don't think it it's fair.”

“We've got these two important Euro games coming up and it doesn't help your confidence and the morale, but we will get over this. We will get over the game and look forward to the next, and we know we need to put together a couple of good results.”

On 2nd April, the international side faced Turkey in a vital Euro 2004 qualifier at Sunderland's Stadium of Light. England's players came in for some strong treatment, David describes the provocation:

"There was some kicking and punching going on and someone even questioned my sexuality. Rio Ferdinand was pinched on the arm in an effort to make him react, but, at the end of the day, they were upset because they had lost the game. They've got a lot of players who get involved in situations but I thought we kept our calm well. It will be probably be hot out there when we play in Turkey but hopefully it will be calm because it's just a football match."

"It was an exceptional performance and we needed it. It was the game which got us going more than anything, as a few of us were hurt by talk of a lack of passion. But if we do our talking on the pitch then there will be no stopping us."

"I thought my booking was harsh but when their players react and come round the referee like they did then sometimes he caves in, but it was a great performance."

"I thought Wayne Rooney was exceptional. I was asked last week whether he was ready to play at this level but he doesn't need me answering any questions for him when he plays the way he did against Turkey." DAVID ON ENGLAND'S NEWEST PRODIGY

The game against Turkey was dogged by racist chanting from some sections of England's supporters. David was at the forefront of the charm offensive before their next match, against Serbia-Montenegro, in June.

MEANWHILE, ON THE PITCH...

"If we had to play a qualifying game behind closed doors that would be sad for football, sad for England and sad for the proper England fans who have to suffer because of the small minority of fans that are doing this. It shouldn't happen but it might just have to happen to stop this."

"The crowd trouble where the supporters came on to the pitch against Turkey was well documented. It shouldn't happen because, if it does happen any more, we will be thrown out of the competition."

"We have to be careful about our celebrations. I don't believe the players were responsible but we have to cut it down. We have to celebrate in the middle of the pitch instead of by the corner flag. We want to stay in the competition."

"I can't imagine a game where there's no crowd. It would be like a pre-season friendly, a practice match. It's a shame for the fans and young kids who are coming to watch players they admire but if it's going to put an end to the trouble then we should consider it."

"It's disappointing when you see some of the trouble that goes on around football matches. There was a period when most of it had stopped but it seems to be creeping back into the game. Of course players notice it and worry about it. We've got family and friends in the stands that come to games."

"Respect has got to be shown to the opposition, especially with the national anthem. Booing a national anthem is disrespectful. Racism, violence and people running on to the pitch has got to be put out of our game. It is going to get us into a lot of trouble."

"Teams fills their grounds because Manchester United are playing. It's a big thing to see their own teams playing against us, that is why we have to go to away ground sand perform."

"We have to remain positive and believe we can catch Arsenal. It's been a weird season because everyone seems to have won and lost a few games."

"We were encouraged by beating the likes of Newcastle, Arsenal and Liverpool but over the past five or six years, we have won the league because we have beaten the lower teams. We have slipped up at times and that has been disappointing."

"I hate being on the bench, whether it is the manager's decision or my own but that is the way it has been for the last couple of months. It doesn't really matter whether you win or lose because you want to be out there doing what you can."

"It was unfortunate that I broke my rib because there was a point when I couldn't even go on a bike."

"The manager has said that he wants me to get ten goals this season and that is what I should be getting. I want to score more and would like to beat the sixteen I got last season."

"It's hard to know how we can beat Juventus and then draw with Bolton, with all due respect to them. It's not an excuse but twelve o'clock kick-offs don't help. We're playing a world-class team on the Wednesday and then coming back to play on the Saturday morning. It's not easy to eat pasta at nine o'clock in the morning, I know that much! That puts you off quite a lot. That's the thing the players don't like."

DAVID ON HOW MIDDAY KICK-OFFS PLAY HAVOC WITH THE BODY CLOCK

MEANWHILE, ON THE PITCH...

❝The whole team is buzzing. I think we are all still on a high because the scale of our achievements is only now sinking in. People had written us off before Christmas and that makes our success even sweeter this time. It has been a tough battle for all of us because we have had to be so focused on our aim to win the league by winning every game and not to worry or get distracted by the opposition. It's been an amazing season for the club and I have never known the team spirit to be as good as it is today. The supporters have been fantastic as always and it's great to reward them with the title.❞ DAVID ON UNITED'S EIGHTH TITLE IN ELEVEN YEARS

David's next international performance was to end less gloriously. On 22nd May, he fractured the scaphoid bone in his wrist during England's friendly in South Africa. The day before, he and the rest of the squad had enjoyed an audience with Nelson Mandela.

❝As England captain I'd like to say this is a great honour for me, the players, the manager and the rest of the FA to meet a man like you. It is an amazing honour for everyone involved.❞

DAVID GREETS THE GREAT MAN

❝I have a promise from David Beckham that he will support our bid. That alone gives us a great deal of hope.❞

NELSON MANDELA ON SOUTH AFRICA'S BID TO HOST THE 2010 WORLD CUP FINALS

❝World Cups are special moments for everyone involved in them. I've been lucky enough to play in two of them and to have it in a country like South Africa would be amazing. Hopefully I will be involved in the next one in Germany in 2006 because that has the potential to be a massive one for England, but if I look after myself and treat my body right, which I have done, then I would love to be there in 2010 leading England into that tournament.❞

"It is definitely important for me to get some sort of break, because for the first time in five or six years I will have four or five weeks off. You always feel tired at the end of a season and it's been quite a hard season with the team having to pull back from a start where we didn't play as well as we can do. The effort all the players have put in takes it out of you but with this break hopefully I'll go back for pre-season being a lot fresher than in past pre-seasons."

WITH NELSON MANDELA AND
SVEN GORAN ERIKSSON

"He went to hospital after suffering the injury, had an X-Ray and it has been confirmed that there is a break." F.A. SPOKESMAN

"I feel really sorry for David because that was his last game of the season and he has got that painful injury. If you gave me one million dollars I couldn't name the bone which he has damaged but I just hope he recovers as quickly as possible so he can have a normal life during the summer."

ENGLAND COACH SVEN-GORAN ERIKSSON OFFERS HIS SYMPATHY

"David Beckham doesn't do ordinary clothes or haircuts – and he doesn't do ordinary injuries either. Less stylish players might strain their groin or tweak a hamstring." THE MIRROR

"David will remain the England captain. I hope he remains captain for a long time. He takes the role unbelievably seriously, which can only be good for the FA and the team."

DAVID DAVIES, F.A'S DIRECTOR OF FOOTBALL OPERATIONS

MEANWHILE, ON THE PITCH...

End It Like Beckham

ON 17TH JUNE 2003, DAVID ENDED MONTHS OF SPECULATION BY SIGNING FOR SPANISH GIANTS REAL MADRID, BREAKING A SIXTEEN-YEAR BOND WITH OLD TRAFFORD THAT HAD LASTED SINCE BOYHOOD

"Manchester United today reached agreement for the transfer of David Beckham to Real Madrid for a fee of 35million euros.**"**
OFFICIAL STATEMENT FROM OLD TRAFFORD

"There exit icons in the world of football and Beckham is one of them." JORE VALDANO TALKS UP HIS MAN

"Beckham, ya**" SPANISH NEWSPAPER HEADLINE THE DAY AFTER**

"Beckham is the Real thing" THE DAILY TELEGRAPH GETS IN ON THE PUNS

"We've been watching from a distance hoping there was a master-plan but, if there was one, it was a master-plan in how to lose £10m.**" OLIVER HOUSTON OF SHAREHOLDERS UNITED VOICES HIS DISAPPROVAL**

"Someone needs to call the police. We've been mugged."
MAN. UTD FAN 'FAT AL' REGISTERS HIS OWN PROTEST ON THE CLUB'S WEBSITE

"It's awful that he's gone. I'm really upset. It's awful for Manchester. Beckham was the only glamour in the Manchester United team. I think the club has treated him terribly. Good luck to him.**"**
ANOTHER FAN'S MESSAGE SUMS UP THE VIEWS OF MANY ON THE WEBSITE

END IT LIKE BECKHAM

"It has come like a great bomb for us, it is a big shock"

BARCELONA'S PRESS OFFICER REGISTERS HIS CLUB'S DISAPPOINTMENT.
THE CATALAN CLUB WERE FAVOURITES AT ONE STAGE FOR DAVID'S SIGNATURE

"I would like to publicly thank Sir Alex Ferguson for making me the player I am today."

"I've known David since he was eleven years of age and it's been a pleasure to see him grow and develop into the player he has become...I would like to wish him and his family every success in the future and thank him for his service to the club."

SIR ALEX RETURNS THE COMPLIMENT

"What was he [Alex Ferguson] doing on holiday in France when the Beckham story came to the boil? It's like he lit a stick of dynamite and scarpered when the fuse was halfway to being blown."

BRIAN CLOUGH

"I will always hold precious memories of my time at Manchester United and Old Trafford as well as the players, who I regard as part of my family, and the brilliant fans who have given me so much support and continue to do so"

"I know that I will always regret it later in life if I had turned down the chance to play at another great club like Real Madrid."

"I wish Manchester United the best of luck and led by such an inspirational captain as Roy Keane, I am sure they will continue to go from strength to strength"

"I would like to thank other clubs who were interested in signing me, including Barcelona...but I really want to play in the Champions League."

"He could put himself up there with Zidane. He could take his own place in Real's folklore." FORMER UNITED BOSS RON ATKINSON

"David has been a credit to the club on and off the pitch and I am surprised and disappointed at the way the club has treated him."

ANOTHER EX-UNITED MANAGER TOMMY DOCHERTY VOICES HIS DISPLEASURE

"What does not make sense for the club is to let top players leave at the end of their contract on a free transfer. In David's case, our approach in mid-May to his advisers about extending his current deal, which had just two years to run, did not meet with an immediate positive response. Around the same time, we were approached by several clubs in Spain and Italy who were

SIGNING FOR REAL MADRID

interested in buying David. We were also told by the player's advisers that they, too, had been contacted by foreign clubs. It was at this point that it became clear a transfer deal involving David might prove beneficial, not only for the club, but also for the player."

UNITED'S CHIEF EXECUTIVE PETER KENYON EXPLAINS HIS DECISION

END IT LIKE BECKHAM

BECKS *Talking*

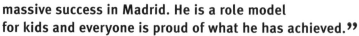

"I just feel that Beckham's superstar status and his superstar wife don't go down too well with Fergie because he likes his players fully focussed on their football the whole time."

FORMER UNITED STAR
PAUL MCGRATH OFFERS A CLUE
TO DAVID'S DEPARTURE

"He is a real East End boy made good and I have no doubt that he will be a massive success in Madrid. He is a role model for kids and everyone is proud of what he has achieved."

EX-ENGLAND INTERNATIONAL AND FELLOW LONDONER TONY COTTEE PAYS TRIBUTE

"He's a celebrity, get him out of here."

DAILY STAR FOOTBALL CORRESPONDENT BRIAN WOOLNOUGH TRIES
TO READ SIR ALEX FERGUSON'S MIND

"The fee has been viewed by some as low, particularly when compared to the money spent by us and other clubs on players in recent years. However, the reality is that in the past twelve months the transfer market has virtually collapsed, with player values falling dramatically. In a depressed market, a fee of up to £25m for a player just two years from the end of his contract represents a good deal." PETER KENYO.

"A ridiculously feminine clothes horse, dominated by a ruthless wife, with one aim. Not to be the best footballer in the world but the most famous face."

THE DAILY MIRROR'S BRIAN READE TAKES A PARTING SWIPE

"When you change club and country you sometimes need time to adjust. Maybe in Spain he will have a little problem in the beginning but I think for the good players it is generally very easy." BRAZILIAN LEGEND PELE

“At the moment the best question is where David is going to play, not where Luis Figo is going to play”

JORGE VALDANO PONDERS A MOUTH-WATERING SELECTION PROBLEM

“**Our relationship with Manchester United is a warm one but it was the strong desire of David to play for Real Madrid that made this all possible.**” JORE VALDANO

“Once I go to Spain to finalise my move and do my medical, I'm going to do a message for the Manchester United fans. They have been a massive part of my life and my career and to just leave without saying anything wouldn't be right. I owe them a lot.”

DAVID SPEAKS FOR THE FIRST TIME ABOUT THE MOVE, 19TH JUNE

“ **I am very excited to become part of Real Madrid. It is going to be a very good challenge for me, on the football field and off it.**”

“Of course I would have been happier if the transfer had been done differently but I don't want to talk about that side of it. I'm a Real player now and I'm looking forward to it.”

“**I understand reports are circulating that I was unhappy with some aspects of my transfer from Manchester United. That is not the case and I did not mean to give that impression in any way. I have publicly expressed my thanks and appreciation for the way the deal has been done by the club, my advisors and Real Madrid. The only thing I was a bit concerned about was the timing – bearing in mind that the Spanish League had not finished.**”

END IT LIKE BECKHAM

❝I want to apologise to the Real players because all this has not been caused by me and I didn't want it to detract from their last two games of the season. They're fighting to win the League and I didn't want anything to upset that. I wish them good luck.❞

❝**I would never think of taking that number off Raul. He is the king of Real Madrid as far as I'm concerned. I haven't discussed the number seven. Whatever number they want to give me I'm happy.**❞ DAVID DISMISSES SPECULATION THAT HE WILL KEEP THE NUMBER 7 SHIRT

❝I wouldn't have done it if it affected my England career. I have spoken to Mr. Eriksson about it and he just said to me 'whatever you do, it doesn't matter what club you are playing for, it doesn't affect you being England captain'.❞

❝**I know a few phrases such as how to order a bill in a restaurant. That will come in handy.**❞

DAVID ANSWERS QUESTIONS ABOUT HIS PROWESS IN SPANISH

❝The more intriguing question for me is not will he play but where will he play... a lot of commentators, including me, have long wanted to see Beckham given a chance to see what he can do in central midfield... one certainty for me is that Beckham will become a much better player.❞ **GARY LINEKER**

Immediately after the transfer was announced, David was whisked away by his new club for a promotional tour of the Far East. His arrival in Tokyo saw 'Beckham-mania' in full swing.

❝Seeing these kids' faces and how happy they are, this just makes my trip.❞

❝**I don't know. Do you have any ideas for me?**❞

DAVID ANSWERS A SCHOOLGIRL'S QUESTION ON WHAT HAIRSTYLE HE IS PLANNING NEXT

"We're out here to greet Beckham. I hope we don't have any ocustomers for lunch today." **A WAITRESS SUMS UP THE MOOD OF THE CITY**

"I am overwhelmed again. It is a great honour and a great pleasure to be here in this country."

"It's amazing to be back in Japan. Arriving at the airport was something special, something we've never seen as a couple."

Meanwhile, back in Spain, Real Madrid's manager Vicente del Bosque was sacked just days after the club were crowned as league champions. In a final twist, United's assistant manager Carlos Queiroz is poached from Old Trafford as his successor.

"It has a come as a shock to me but Real Madrid winning the title has made me feel so excited about getting over there, meeting the players and playing, I just hope that I will be as successful with them as I was with Manchester United."

"David is a great player and a great professional. He showed that when he was at United. I always think the best football is played by the best players and I will be trying to make sure they work in harmony. The only time I want to leave Beckham or Luis Figo on the bench is when they are injured." QUEIROZ DISCUSSES A POSSIBLE SELECTION PROBLEM

David finally signed on 1st July after passing a stringent medical. His arrival in Madrid was accompanied by huge crowds and the usual media frenzy.

"It's a bit over the top, he's got more bodyguards than the king"

A SPANISH AUTOGRAPH HUNTER SHOWS HER FRUSTRATION

"The Beckham earthquake arrives today. His arrival is one of our country's most important events for years."

SPANISH SPORTS DAILY MARCA

"I don't understand it. He has all that money and he wears broken trousers."

ONE OF MARCA'S FEMALE STAFF DISAPPROVES OF
DAVID'S RIPPED JEANS

"He has passed. There is nothing to stop him playing for Real Madrid. In our opinion he's in perfect condition."

CLUB DOCTOR ALFONSO DEL CORRAL

"He's slim and strong, looks after himself to the maximum and has not suffered important injuries...he's healthy and strong as a bull." DEL CORRAL

"The team will now have two good-looking players. Until now, I was the only one." REAL'S BRAZILIAN FULL-BACK ROBERTO CARLOS

END IT LIKE BECKHAM

"Competition in a team is always a healthy thing to have and it just means that only those who are sharpest will get to play, but I'm sure they're will be room for everyone, and that includes Beckham." **RONALDO**

"The thing I like about Beckham is his attitude, He is a technical player but he also has the desire to work hard for his team."
REAL'S FULL-BACK SALGADO

"He's so handsome. He's a wonderful player and I'm so thrilled he's signed for us." **14-YEAR-OLD FAN LETITIA OCANA**

"I'm looking forward to the challenge on the field and living in Spain has always interested me so I'm looking forward to it. It's going to be an honour playing for Real and it's such an exciting experience for me. There were a couple of clubs interested. There was Barcelona but also AC Milan and Inter but Real was the only one that really interested me. I've spent thirteen or fourteen years at Man. United. It's been a massive part of my life and will always be but I have to move on as well as Man. United. I'm going to miss the players, particularly the ones I grew up with. It is really hard because I regard all the players as family and to be leaving like this is sad for me but I'll move on."

"Beckham is here because we believe in him as a footballer. David, welcome to the dream League." **REAL'S PRESIDENT FLORENTINO PEREZ**

"I have always loved football. Of course I love my family. I have a wonderful life but football is everything to me and joining Real Madrid is a dream come true. I would like to say thank you to everyone coming and joining me in my arrival. Gracias – hala Madrid." DAVID TRIES OUT HIS SPANISH FOR THE FIRST TIME

"Despite all that's going on, we're not going to lose sight of the fact that we're unveiling this great player. He is a great player who is going to become part of the club's great history. He is a man of our

END IT LIKE BECKHAM

times and a symbol of modern-day stardom and what is certain is Real have signed Beckham because he's a great footballer and a very dedicated professional. His team spirit is unsurpassed and he is one of the best English players of all time and if only because of that he is with us. We love Beckham because he makes us the best team on and off the pitch.** FLORENTINO PEREZ

"It is fantastic that David Beckham has signed for Real Madrid and we will all make him welcome. I am looking forward to playing alongside him and I think he will be happy at Madrid." RONALDO

"Well, Michael Jordan hasn't done too badly with No 23.**"**
VICTORIA HAS THE FINAL SAY IN CHOOSING DAVID'S NEW SHIRT NUMBER